THE 1200-CALORIE WEIGHT LOSS PLAN FOR WOMEN

A Complete 60-Day Slim Down Solution with Simple, Tasty Recipes for Busy Moms - Inspired by Dr. Nowzaradan's Proven Method

© Copyright 2025 – Madeleine Pan. All rights reserved.

Published by Kwon Royalty Publishing, under its Tasty Shelf imprint.

The content contained within this book may not be reproduced, duplicated, or transmitted without direct written permission from the author or the publisher. Under no circumstances will any blame or legal responsibility be held against the publisher or author for any damages, reparation, or monetary loss due to the information contained within this book, either directly or indirectly.

Legal Notice:
This book is copyright protected. It is only for personal use. You cannot amend, distribute, sell, use, quote, or paraphrase any part of the content within this book without the consent of the author or publisher.

Disclaimer Notice:
Please note that the information contained within this document is for educational and entertainment purposes only. All efforts have been executed to present accurate, up-to-date, reliable, and complete information. No warranties of any kind are declared or implied. This book is not affiliated with, Dr. Nowzaradan. The recipes and meal plans are inspired by his dietary principles and designed to support individuals seeking a structured, calorie-conscious eating plan. Please consult a licensed professional before attempting any techniques outlined in this book. By reading this document, the reader agrees that under no circumstances is the author responsible for any losses, direct or indirect, that are incurred as a result of the use of the information contained within this document, including, but not limited to, errors, omissions, or inaccuracies.

All recipes in this cookbook were tested and enjoyed by chefs and cooking enthusiasts to ensure quality, clarity, and real-world results.

GET YOUR FREE EXCLUSIVE BONUSES NOW

DOWNLOAD FOR FREE – SIMPLY SCAN THE QR CODE BELOW!

BONUS 1 — 60-DAY MEAL PLAN

BONUS 2 — SHOPPING LIST

BONUS 3 — MEDITERRANEAN DIET RECIPE E-BOOK

Contents

Why 1200 Calories? 7
Why I Started The 1200-Calorie Diet Plan 8

Breakfast 10
Egg Whites With Spinach & Tomatoes 11
Nonfat Greek Yogurt With Cinnamon & Berries 12
Zucchini & Egg White Frittata 13a
Cabbage & Mushroom Omelet 14
Lean Turkey Breakfast Hash 15
Broccoli & Egg White Bake 16
Lean Turkey & Cauliflower Hash 17
Low-Carb Cottage Cheese Pancakes 18
Smoked Salmon & Egg White Scramble 19
Asparagus & Tomato Egg Muffins 20
High-Protein Scrambled Tofu Bowl 21
Spaghetti Squash & Lean Chicken Hash 22
Garlic Mushroom & Egg White Stir-Fry 23
Baked Egg Whites With Herbs & Veggies 24
Cottage Cheese & Cucumber Protein Bowl 25
Lean Turkey & Bell Pepper Breakfast Wrap 26
Grilled Tomato & Nonfat Cottage Cheese Bowl 27
Zucchini & Egg White Breakfast Muffins 28
Steamed Broccoli & Scrambled Tofu Plate 29
Cauliflower Rice Porridge With Nonfat Yogurt 30

Lunch 31
Grilled Chicken Salad With Lemon Vinaigrette 32
Turkey Lettuce Wraps With Mustard 33
Cauliflower & Lean Chicken Stir-Fry 34
Spicy Egg White & Mushroom Scramble Bowl 35
Zucchini Noodles With Garlic & Shrimp 36
Broccoli & Turkey Soup 37
Tuna & Cucumber Salad With Mustard Dressing 38
Turkey & Spinach Stuffed Bell Peppers 39
Grilled Fish With Lemon & Steamed Veggies 40
Cabbage Slaw With Grilled Chicken Strips 41
Mushroom & Tofu Stir-Fry With Garlic 42
Lemon Herb Turkey Skewers With Zucchini 43
Steamed Tilapia With Spinach & Vinegar Dressing 44
Cauliflower Rice Sushi With Lean Tuna 45
Zesty Grilled Shrimp With Cabbage Slaw 46
Low-Carb Greek Chicken Salad 47

Grilled Chicken & Cucumber Lettuce Wraps 48
Steamed Shrimp With Zucchini & Garlic Sauce 49
Grilled Tilapia With Spinach & Lemon Dressing 50
Spicy Ground Turkey & Broccoli Bowl 51

Dinner 52

Lemon Garlic Baked Cod With Broccoli 53
Roasted Tilapia With Cabbage & Herb Dressing 54
Low-Carb Turkey & Cabbage Slaw Stir-Fry 55
Lean Chicken Stir-Fry With Bok Choy 56
Grilled Turkey & Mushroom Skewers 57
Baked Lemon Chicken With Cauliflower Rice 58
Spaghetti Squash & Shrimp Bowl 59
Steamed Fish With Asparagus & Vinegar Dressing 60
Garlic & Herb Turkey Meatballs 61
Baked Turkey & Zucchini Meatloaf 62
Nonfat Cottage Cheese & Cucumber Protein Plate 63
Lean Chicken & Cabbage Spring Rolls 64
Roasted Salmon With Lemon & Zucchini 65
Cabbage Stir-Fry With Garlic Shrimp 66
Low-Carb Ground Turkey Lettuce Tacos 67
Oven-Baked Fish With Garlic & Herbs 68
Spaghetti Squash With Chicken & Tomato Sauce 69
Broccoli & Turkey Casserole 70
Herb-Crusted Baked Tilapia With Cauliflower Mash 71
Lemon Pepper Grilled Chicken With Cabbage Slaw 72
Zucchini Noodles With Lean Ground Turkey 73
Baked Turkey Meatballs With Roasted Asparagus 74
Zesty Lemon Pepper Fish With Roasted Cauliflower 75
Savory Chicken & Mushroom Skillet 76
Mustard Glazed Chicken With Zucchini Medley 77

Drinks 78

Cabbage & Cucumber Detox Juice 79
Nonfat Yogurt & Strawberry Protein Shake 80
Unsweetened Hibiscus Iced Tea With Lemon 81
Spinach & Cucumber Green Juice 82
Herbal Lemon-Ginger Detox Tea 83
60-Day Meal Plan and Shopping List 84
Week 1 84
Week 2 86
Week 3 88
Week 4 90
Week 5 92
Week 6 94
Week 7 96
Week 8 98

WHY 1200 CALORIES?

Unlock the Smart, Sustainable Path to Weight Loss

When it comes to lasting weight loss, one of the most effective strategies is calorie control — and the 1200-calorie diet has emerged as a proven standard for women seeking real, sustainable results. This calorie level is low enough to promote steady fat loss, yet carefully balanced to ensure you still receive essential nutrients, energy, and satisfaction from your meals. It's not about starving — it's about strategic, smarter eating.

This cookbook is inspired by the approach popularized by Dr. Younan Nowzaradan (Dr. Now), a renowned bariatric surgeon known for helping patients achieve dramatic weight loss through structured, practical plans. His 1200-calorie method has helped thousands kickstart their health journey by focusing on lean proteins, non-starchy vegetables, and eliminating processed carbs, sugars, and high-fat foods.

Inside, you'll find delicious, budget-friendly recipes and a complete 60-day meal plan tailored to help you stay full, boost your energy, and burn fat — without sacrificing flavor or spending hours in the kitchen. Whether you're just beginning your wellness journey or need a simple plan to stay on track, this cookbook will help you feel stronger, healthier, and more confident — one satisfying meal at a time.

WHY I STARTED THE 1200-CALORIE DIET PLAN

Like many women, I found myself trapped in a frustrating cycle—losing a few pounds with every new fad diet, only to gain them right back. I tried everything: trendy detoxes, restrictive meal plans, complicated macros, and intense workouts. Nothing stuck. I was tired, drained, and looking for something that was actually realistic.

That's when I discovered the 1200-calorie meal plan: a simple, structured approach that focuses on lean proteins, fresh veggies, and whole foods—without expensive gimmicks or starvation. It made sense, and more importantly, it worked.

I was skeptical at first, but once I got started, I felt more in control, more energized, and never deprived. This plan didn't just help me lose weight—it helped me finally break free from the dieting rollercoaster.

Adapting to the 1200-Calorie Limit

The biggest challenge was learning to work with the calorie restriction without feeling deprived. I had to completely rethink my meals—portion sizes, ingredient choices, and even my approach to hunger.

Meal planning became my best friend. Instead of grabbing whatever was convenient, I started preparing meals ahead of time, making sure every bite counted. I focused on lean proteins, non-starchy vegetables, and low-carb meals, which allowed me to eat more volume while keeping my calorie count in check.

Portion control was another hurdle. Before this diet, I overestimated what a "healthy portion" actually looked like. It was a wake-up call when I measured out my first serving of chicken and realized how much I had been overeating—even with healthy foods. But as I adjusted, I began to appreciate quality over quantity.

Of course, cravings didn't magically disappear. There were moments when I desperately wanted to reach for sugary snacks or carb-heavy comfort foods. The trick was finding smart alternatives—a well-seasoned cauliflower mash instead of mashed potatoes, a protein-rich Greek yogurt in place of ice cream. Over time, these swaps became second nature, and I stopped feeling like I was missing out.

Results & Key Takeaways

The results? Life-changing.
Within just a few weeks, I noticed a difference—not just on the scale, but in my energy levels, my cravings, and even my mindset around food. My body felt lighter, my digestion improved, and my cravings for unhealthy foods gradually faded.

Beyond the physical transformation, what surprised me most was how sustainable this diet felt. Unlike extreme weight loss programs that demand unrealistic sacrifices, Dr. Now's approach was about long-term success, not temporary deprivation.

Key Lessons I Learned:
- Food should fuel your body, not control it. Learning to eat with purpose made all the difference.
- Planning is everything. When you have a strategy in place, there's no room for impulsive, unhealthy choices.
- It gets easier. The first few days were tough, but by week two, it became my new normal.

If you're considering this diet, know that it's absolutely possible. Yes, it takes commitment, but with the right meals and mindset, you won't just lose weight—you'll gain control over your health.

BREAKFAST

EGG WHITES WITH SPINACH & TOMATOES

INGREDIENTS

- 6 egg whites
- 1 cup fresh spinach, chopped
- ½ cup cherry tomatoes, halved
- ½ tsp garlic powder
- ¼ tsp black pepper
- ½ tsp dried oregano
- 1 tsp apple cider vinegar
- 1 tbsp water

PREP TIME: 5 MINS **COOK TIME:** 10 MINS **SERVING:** 2

INSTRUCTIONS

1. Whisk the egg whites in a bowl until slightly frothy, then add garlic powder, black pepper, and oregano for flavor.
2. Heat a non-stick skillet on moderate heat and add the water. Once warm, toss in the spinach and let it wilt for 1-2 minutes, stirring occasionally.
3. Add the cherry tomatoes and cook for another minute until they start to soften.
4. Pour in the egg whites evenly over the vegetables, making sure they spread across the pan. Let them cook undisturbed for 2-3 minutes until the edges begin to set.
5. Gently fold the eggs with a spatula and continue cooking for another 2-3 minutes, stirring occasionally to ensure even cooking.
6. Drizzle apple cider vinegar over the eggs just before serving to enhance the flavor. Serve immediately.

Storage & Reheating:

Refrigeration: Store in an airtight container for up to 2 days.
Freezing: Not recommended.
Reheating: Microwave for 30-60 seconds, stirring halfway through.

Nutrition

Calories: 110, **Fat:** 1g, **Cholesterol:** 0mg, **Carbohydrates:** 4g, **Sugar:** 2g, **Protein:** 22g, **Sodium:** 180mg, **Fiber:** 1g

NONFAT GREEK YOGURT WITH CINNAMON & BERRIES

INGREDIENTS

- 1 cup nonfat Greek yogurt (plain, unsweetened)
- ½ cup mixed berries (strawberries, raspberries, blueberries)
- ½ tsp ground cinnamon
- ½ tsp vanilla extract (optional)

PREP TIME: 5 MINS **COOK TIME:** 00 MINS **SERVING:** 2

INSTRUCTIONS

1. Scoop the Greek yogurt into the shallow bowl and sprinkle the cinnamon on top.
2. Gently fold the cinnamon into the yogurt to evenly distribute the flavor.
3. Add the mixed berries on top, slightly pressing them into the yogurt.
4. Drizzle vanilla extract (if using) and lightly mix before serving.

Nutrition
Calories: 90, **Fat:** 0g, **Cholesterol:** 5mg, **Carbohydrates:** 9g, **Sugar:** 6g, **Protein:** 14g, **Sodium:** 60mg, **Fiber:** 2g

Storage & Reheating:

Refrigeration: Store in an airtight container for up to 3 days.
Freezing: Not recommended.
Reheating: Not needed.

ZUCCHINI & EGG WHITE FRITTATA

INGREDIENTS

- 6 egg whites
- 1 small zucchini, thinly sliced
- ½ small onion, finely chopped
- ½ tsp garlic powder
- ¼ tsp black pepper
- ½ tsp dried basil
- 1 tsp apple cider vinegar
- 1 tbsp water

PREP TIME: 10 MINS **COOK TIME:** 20 MINS **SERVING:** 2

INSTRUCTIONS

1. Preheat oven to 375°F (190°C).
2. Heat a non-stick skillet on moderate heat. Add the onion and zucchini and toss with the water. Cook for 3-4 minutes until softened.
3. Whisk the egg whites in a deep-bottom bowl with garlic powder, black pepper, and basil.
4. Pour the egg white mixture over the cooked vegetables in the skillet and let it set for 2-3 minutes without stirring.
5. Transfer the skillet and bake for 15 minutes until the frittata is fully set and slightly golden on top.
6. Drizzle apple cider vinegar before serving to enhance the flavor. Slice and serve warm.

Nutrition
Calories: 120, **Fat:** 1g, **Cholesterol:** 0mg, **Carbohydrates:** 5g, **Sugar:** 2g, **Protein:** 22g, **Sodium:** 160mg, **Fiber:** 1g

Storage & Reheating:

Refrigeration: Store in an airtight container for up to 3 days.
Freezing: Not recommended.
Reheating: Microwave for 30-60 seconds or reheat on moderate heat on the stovetop.

CABBAGE & MUSHROOM OMELET

INGREDIENTS

- 6 egg whites
- 1 cup cabbage, finely shredded
- ½ cup mushrooms, sliced
- ½ tsp garlic powder
- ¼ tsp black pepper
- ½ tsp dried parsley
- 1 tbsp water

Nutrition

Calories: 110, **Fat:** 1g, **Cholesterol:** 0mg, **Carbohydrates:** 5g, **Sugar:** 2g, **Protein:** 22g, **Sodium:** 140mg, **Fiber:** 2g

 PREP TIME: 10 MINS   **COOK TIME:** 10 MINS   **SERVING:** 2

INSTRUCTIONS

1. Whisk the egg whites in a deep-bottom bowl, adding garlic powder, black pepper, and dried parsley. Set aside.
2. Heat a non-stick skillet on moderate heat. Add the shredded cabbage and mushrooms with 1 tbsp of water and toss to combine. Sauté for 3-4 minutes until softened.
3. Ladle in the egg whites, ensuring they spread evenly across the pan.
4. Let it cook undisturbed for 3 minutes, then softly lift the edges and tilt the pan to allow any uncooked egg whites to flow underneath.
5. Fold the omelet in half and cook for more 2 minutes until fully set.
6. Serve warm, optionally garnishing with extra parsley.

Storage & Reheating:

Refrigeration: Store in an airtight container for up to 2 days.
Freezing: Not recommended.
Reheating: Microwave for 30-45 seconds or reheat on moderate heat in a skillet.

LEAN TURKEY BREAKFAST HASH

INGREDIENTS

- 200g lean ground turkey (93% lean or higher)
- 1 cup cauliflower rice (fresh or frozen)
- ½ cup diced onions
- ½ tsp paprika
- ½ tsp garlic powder
- ½ tsp black pepper
- 2 tbsp water (for sautéing)

PREP TIME: 10 MINS   **COOK TIME:** 12 MINS   **SERVING:** 2

INSTRUCTIONS

1. Heat a non-stick skillet on moderate heat. Add the diced onions and 1 tablespoon of water. Sauté for 2–3 minutes until they begin to soften.
2. Add the ground turkey and break it apart with a spatula. Cook for 5–6 minutes, stirring occasionally, until fully browned and cooked through.
3. Add the cauliflower rice, paprika, garlic powder, black pepper, and another tablespoon of water.
4. Stir well and cook for another 3–4 minutes until the cauliflower is tender and everything is heated through.
5. Serve hot. Optional: garnish with chopped parsley or extra paprika.

Nutrition
Calories: 210, **Fat:** 8g, **Cholesterol:** 55mg, **Carbohydrates:** 4g, **Sugar:** 2g, **Protein:** 28g, **Sodium:** 85mg, **Fiber:** 2g

Storage & Reheating:

Refrigeration: Store in an airtight container for up to 3 days.
Freezing: Freeze in individual portions for up to 1 month.
Reheating: Microwave for 1–2 minutes or reheat in a skillet on low heat.

BROCCOLI & EGG WHITE BAKE

INGREDIENTS

- 6 egg whites
- 1 cup broccoli florets, chopped
- ½ tsp garlic powder
- ¼ tsp black pepper
- ½ tsp dried oregano
- 1 tbsp water

PREP TIME: 10 MINS **COOK TIME:** 25 MINS **SERVING:** 2

INSTRUCTIONS

1. Preheat oven to 375°F (190°C).
2. Lightly grease a baking dish with a tiny amount of water and toss in the chopped broccoli.
3. Whisk the egg whites in a deep-bottom bowl, adding garlic powder, black pepper, and oregano.
4. Drop the egg white mixture evenly over the broccoli in the baking dish.
5. Bake in a preheated oven at 375°F (190°C) for 18–20 minutes, or until the center is just set. This is a soft bake — avoid overbaking if you prefer a tender finish over a browned top.
6. Remove from the oven, let it cool for 2 minutes, then slice and serve warm.

Nutrition

Calories: 120, **Fat:** 1g, **Cholesterol:** 0mg, **Carbohydrates:** 5g, **Sugar:** 2g, **Protein:** 22g, **Sodium:** 160mg, **Fiber:** 2g

Storage & Reheating:

Refrigeration: Store in an airtight for up to 3 days.
Freezing: Not recommended.
Reheating: Microwave for 30-60 seconds or reheat on moderate heat in the oven.

LEAN TURKEY & CAULIFLOWER HASH

INGREDIENTS

- 200g lean ground turkey
- 1 cup cauliflower, finely chopped
- ½ cup onions, diced
- ½ tsp garlic powder
- ¼ tsp black pepper
- ½ tsp dried thyme
- 1 tbsp water

PREP TIME: 10 MINS **COOK TIME:** 15 MINS **SERVING:** 2

INSTRUCTIONS

1. Heat a non-stick skillet on moderate heat. Add the diced onions and 1 tbsp of water. Cook for 2-3 minutes until softened.
2. Add the ground turkey, breaking it up with a spatula, and cook for 5-6 minutes until browned.
3. Toss in the cauliflower, garlic powder, black pepper, and thyme. Stir well to combine.
4. Continue cooking for more 5 minutes, stirring at intervals, until the cauliflower softens and absorbs the flavors.
5. Serve hot, garnished with extra thyme if desired.

Nutrition
Calories: 180, **Fat:** 4g, **Cholesterol:** 45mg, **Carbohydrates:** 6g, **Sugar:** 2g, **Protein:** 28g, **Sodium:** 180mg, **Fiber:** 2g

Storage & Reheating:

Refrigeration: Store in an airtight container for up to 3 days.
Freezing: Freeze in a meal prep container for up to 3 months.
Reheating: Microwave for 1-2 minutes or reheat on moderate heat in a skillet.

LOW-CARB COTTAGE CHEESE PANCAKES

INGREDIENTS

- ½ cup nonfat cottage cheese
- 3 egg whites
- ¼ cup oat flour
- ½ tsp vanilla extract (optional)
- ½ tsp cinnamon
- ½ tsp baking powder

PREP TIME: 15 MINS **COOK TIME:** 15 MINS **SERVING:** 2

INSTRUCTIONS

1. Blend the cottage cheese, egg whites, oat flour, vanilla extract, cinnamon, and baking powder until their texture turns smooth.
2. Heat a non-stick skillet on moderate heat and ladle small portions of the batter onto the skillet.
3. Cook for 2-3 minutes until bubbles appear on the top surface, then flip and cook for more 2 minutes until golden brown.
4. Serve warm, optionally topping with a sprinkle of extra cinnamon.

Nutrition
Calories: 140, **Fat:** 1g, **Cholesterol:** 10mg, **Carbohydrates:** 12g, **Sugar:** 3g, **Protein:** 18g, **Sodium:** 160mg, **Fiber:** 2g

Storage & Reheating:

Refrigeration: Store in an airtight container for up to 3 days.
Freezing: Freeze for up to 2 months.
Reheating: Microwave for 30 seconds or reheat on moderate heat in a skillet.

SMOKED SALMON & EGG WHITE SCRAMBLE

INGREDIENTS

- 6 egg whites
- 50g smoked salmon, chopped
- ½ cup spinach, chopped
- ½ tsp garlic powder
- ¼ tsp black pepper
- ½ tsp dried dill
- 1 tbsp water

PREP TIME: 10 MINS

COOK TIME: 10 MINS

SERVING: 2

INSTRUCTIONS

1. Whisk the egg whites in a deep-bottom bowl, adding garlic powder, black pepper, and dried dill. Set aside.
2. Heat a non-stick skillet on moderate heat. Add the spinach and 1 tbsp water. Cook for 1-2 minutes until wilted.
3. Ladle in the egg whites and let them cook (don't run spatula this time) for 2-3 minutes, allowing them to set slightly.
4. Gently stir it with a spatula, breaking it into soft curds.
5. Add smoked salmon and cook for more 1-2 minutes, just until warmed through.
6. Serve immediately, garnished with extra dill if desired.

Nutrition

Calories: 150, **Fat:** 2g, **Cholesterol:** 20mg, **Carbohydrates:** 3g, **Sugar:** 1g, **Protein:** 30g, **Sodium:** 320mg, **Fiber:** 1g

Storage & Reheating:

Refrigeration: Store in an airtight container for up to 2 days.
Freezing: Not recommended.
Reheating: Microwave for 30-45 seconds, stirring halfway through.

ASPARAGUS & TOMATO EGG MUFFINS

INGREDIENTS

- 6 egg whites
- ½ cup asparagus, chopped
- ½ cup cherry tomatoes, diced
- ½ tsp garlic powder
- ¼ tsp black pepper
- ½ tsp dried basil

 PREP TIME: 10 MINS   **COOK TIME:** 20 MINS   **SERVING:** 2

INSTRUCTIONS

1. Preheat oven to 375°F (190°C).
2. Whisk the egg whites in a deep-bottom bowl with garlic powder, black pepper, and basil.
3. Divide the chopped asparagus and cherry tomatoes evenly into a lightly greased muffin tin.
4. Pour the egg white mixture over the vegetables, filling each muffin cup about ¾ full.
5. Bake for 18-20 minutes or until the muffins are fully set and slightly golden on top.
6. Remove and let them cool for 2 minutes before serving.

Nutrition
Calories: 110, **Fat:** 1g, **Cholesterol:** 0mg, **Carbohydrates:** 5g, **Sugar:** 2g, **Protein:** 22g, **Sodium:** 140mg, **Fiber:** 1g

Storage & Reheating:

Refrigeration: Store in an airtight container for up to 3 days.
Freezing: Not recommended.
Reheating: Microwave for 30-45 seconds.

HIGH-PROTEIN SCRAMBLED TOFU BOWL

INGREDIENTS

- 200g firm tofu, crumbled
- ½ cup bell peppers, diced
- ½ cup onions, chopped
- ½ tsp turmeric powder
- ¼ tsp black pepper
- ½ tsp garlic powder
- 1 tbsp water

PREP TIME: 10 MINS	**COOK TIME:** 12 MINS	**SERVING:** 2

INSTRUCTIONS

1. Heat a non-stick skillet on moderate heat. Add the onions, bell peppers, and one tbsp water. Sauté for 3-4 minutes until softened.
2. Add crumbled tofu and powder it with turmeric, black pepper, and garlic powder.
3. Stir constantly for 5-6 minutes, letting the tofu absorb the flavors and develop a golden color.
4. Cook for an additional 2 minutes, stirring with intervals, until everything is well combined and heated through.
5. Serve warm, optionally garnished with extra black pepper.

Nutrition
Calories: 140, **Fat:** 4g, **Cholesterol:** 0mg, **Carbohydrates:** 6g, **Sugar:** 2g, **Protein:** 18g, **Sodium:** 130mg, **Fiber:** 2g

Storage & Reheating:

Refrigeration: Store in an airtight container for up to 3 days.
Freezing: Not recommended.
Reheating: Microwave for 30-60 seconds or reheat on moderate heat in a skillet.

SPAGHETTI SQUASH & LEAN CHICKEN HASH

INGREDIENTS

- 1 cup spaghetti squash, cooked & shredded
- 150g skinless chicken breast, diced
- ½ cup onions, diced
- ½ tsp garlic powder
- ¼ tsp black pepper
- ½ tsp dried thyme
- 1 tbsp water

 PREP TIME: 10 MINS   **COOK TIME:** 15 MINS   **SERVING:** 2

INSTRUCTIONS

1. Put the high-edge, non-stick skillet on moderate heat. Add the onions and one tablespoon of water. Sauté for 2-3 minutes until softened.
2. Add diced meat and cook for 5-6 minutes, stirring at intervals, until browned and fully cooked.
3. Toss in the spaghetti squash, garlic powder, black pepper, and thyme. Stir well to combine.
4. Cook for more than 5 minutes, stirring occasionally, until everything is well blended and heated through.
5. Serve immediately, garnished with extra thyme if desired.

Nutrition
Calories: 180, **Fat:** 3g, **Cholesterol:** 45mg, **Carbohydrates:** 7g, **Sugar:** 2g, **Protein:** 30g, **Sodium:** 180mg, **Fiber:** 2g

Storage & Reheating:

Refrigeration: Store in an airtight wide-mouth large jar for up to 3 days.

Freezing: Freeze in a meal prep container for up to 3 months.

Reheating: Microwave for 1-2 minutes or reheat on moderate heat in a skillet.

GARLIC MUSHROOM & EGG WHITE STIR-FRY

INGREDIENTS

- 6 egg whites
- 1 cup mushrooms, sliced
- ½ cup onions, diced
- ½ tsp garlic powder
- ¼ tsp black pepper
- ½ tsp dried parsley
- 1 tbsp water

 PREP TIME: 10 MINS   **COOK TIME:** 12 MINS   **SERVING:** 2

INSTRUCTIONS

1. Heat a non-stick skillet on moderate heat. Add the onions, mushrooms, and 1 tablespoon of water. Sauté for 3–4 minutes until softened.
2. In a deep-bottom bowl, whisk the egg whites with garlic powder, black pepper, and dried parsley until well combined.
3. Ladle the seasoned egg whites into the skillet. Let them cook undisturbed for 2–3 minutes, allowing them to set slightly.
4. Gently stir the eggs, breaking them into soft curds. Cook for more than 2 minutes until fully set.
5. Serve warm, with extra parsley sprinkled on top if desired.

Nutrition

Calories: 120, **Fat:** 1g, **Cholesterol:** 0mg, **Carbohydrates:** 5g, **Sugar:** 2g, **Protein:** 22g, **Sodium:** 160mg, **Fiber:** 1g

Storage & Reheating:

Refrigeration: Store in an airtight container for up to 2 days.
Freezing: Not recommended.
Reheating: Microwave for 30-45 seconds or reheat on moderate heat in a skillet.

BAKED EGG WHITES WITH HERBS & VEGGIES

INGREDIENTS

- 6 egg whites
- ½ cup bell peppers, diced
- ½ cup zucchini, finely chopped
- ½ cup mushrooms, sliced
- ½ tsp garlic powder
- ¼ tsp black pepper
- ½ tsp dried parsley

 PREP TIME: 10 MINS   **COOK TIME:** 20 MINS   **SERVING:** 2

INSTRUCTIONS

1. Preheat oven to 375°F (190°C).
2. Lightly grease a baking dish with a tiny amount of water and toss in the bell peppers, zucchini, and mushrooms.
3. Whisk the egg whites in a deep-bottom bowl, adding garlic powder, black pepper, and parsley.
4. Drop egg white mixture over the veggies, ensuring an even spread.
5. Bake for 18-20 minutes until the eggs are fully set.
6. Remove and let cool for 2 minutes, then slice and serve warm.

Nutrition
Calories: 120, **Fat:** 1g, **Cholesterol:** 0mg, **Carbohydrates:** 6g, **Sugar:** 2g, **Protein:** 22g, **Sodium:** 160mg, **Fiber:** 2g

Storage & Reheating:

Refrigeration: Store in an airtight container for up to 3 days.
Freezing: Not recommended.
Reheating: Microwave for 30-60 seconds or reheat on moderate heat in the oven.

COTTAGE CHEESE & CUCUMBER PROTEIN BOWL

INGREDIENTS

- 1 cup nonfat cottage cheese
- ½ cup cucumber, diced
- ½ tsp black pepper
- ½ tsp dried dill

 PREP TIME: 5 MINS   **COOK TIME:** 00 MINS   **SERVING:** 2

INSTRUCTIONS

1. Scoop the nonfat cottage cheese into a serving bowl.
2. Add the diced cucumbers and gently mix.
3. Sprinkle black pepper and dry dill evenly over the top.
4. Serve immediately, or let it chill for extra freshness.

Nutrition

Calories: 100, **Fat:** 0g, **Cholesterol:** 10mg, **Carbohydrates:** 4g, **Sugar:** 3g, **Protein:** 14g, **Sodium:** 400mg, **Fiber:** 0.5g

Storage & Reheating:

Refrigeration: Store in the wide-mouth airtight container for up to 3 days.

Freezing: Not recommended.

Reheating: Not needed.

LEAN TURKEY & BELL PEPPER BREAKFAST WRAP

INGREDIENTS

- 150g lean ground turkey
- ½ cup bell peppers, diced
- ½ cup onions, finely chopped
- 1 egg white wrap (or lettuce for a low-carb option)
- ½ tsp garlic powder
- ¼ tsp black pepper
- ½ tsp dried oregano

PREP TIME: 10 MINS **COOK TIME:** 100 MINS **SERVING:** 2

INSTRUCTIONS

1. Heat a non-stick skillet on moderate heat. Add onions and bell peppers (diced form) and toss to combine. Sauté for 3-4 minutes until softened.
2. Add minced turkey and break it up with a spatula while cooking. Stir occasionally for 5-6 minutes until browned.
3. Sprinkle in the garlic powder, crushed pepper, and oregano, and stir well.
4. Remove and put aside to let the mixture cool for 1 minute.
5. Spoon the turkey mixture into the egg white wrap (or lettuce leaves for a lower-carb option).
6. Wrap tightly and serve warm.

Nutrition

Calories: 180, **Fat:** 3g, **Cholesterol:** 35mg, **Carbohydrates:** 6g, **Sugar:** 2g, **Protein:** 28g, **Sodium:** 200mg, **Fiber:** 1g

Storage & Reheating:

Refrigeration: Store in an airtight container for up to 2 days.
Freezing: Not recommended.
Reheating: Microwave for 30-45 seconds.

GRILLED TOMATO & NONFAT COTTAGE CHEESE BOWL

INGREDIENTS

- 1 cup nonfat cottage cheese
- ½ cup cherry tomatoes, halved
- ½ tsp black pepper
- ½ tsp dried basil

 PREP TIME: 10 MINS   **COOK TIME:** 5 MINS   **SERVING:** 2

INSTRUCTIONS

1. Heat a non-stick skillet on moderate heat. Toss in the cherry tomatoes. Grill for 2-3 minutes until they soften slightly.
2. Scoop the cottage cheese into the shallow bowl and top with the grilled tomatoes.
3. Sprinkle black pepper and dried basil for extra flavor.
4. Serve immediately and enjoy.

Nutrition
Calories: 100, **Fat:** 1g, **Cholesterol:** 5mg, **Carbohydrates:** 5g, **Sugar:** 3g, **Protein:** 14g, **Sodium:** 170mg, **Fiber:** 1g

Storage & Reheating:

Refrigeration: Store in an airtight container for up to 2 days.
Freezing: Instant eating only.
Reheating: Take it as it is.

ZUCCHINI & EGG WHITE BREAKFAST MUFFINS

INGREDIENTS

- 6 egg whites
- ½ cup zucchini, grated
- ½ cup mushrooms, finely chopped
- ½ tsp garlic powder
- ¼ tsp black pepper
- ½ tsp dried thyme

 PREP TIME: 10 MINS   **COOK TIME:** 20 MINS   **SERVING:** 2

INSTRUCTIONS

1. Preheat oven to 375°F (190°C).
2. Lightly grease a muffin tin with a tiny amount of water to prevent sticking.
3. Grate the zucchini with the help of a paper towel to squeeze out excess moisture.
4. Whisk the egg whites in a deep-bottom bowl, adding garlic powder, black pepper, and thyme.
5. Divide the zucchini and mushrooms evenly into the muffin cups.
6. Drop egg white mixture over the veggies, filling each cup about ¾ full.
7. Bake for 18-20 minutes or until the muffins are fully set.
8. Remove and put them aside to let cool for 2 minutes before serving.

Storage & Reheating:

Refrigeration: Store in an airtight wide-mouth jar for up to 3 days.
Freezing: Not recommended.
Reheating: Microwave for 30-45 seconds.

Nutrition
Calories: 110, **Fat:** 1g, **Cholesterol:** 0mg, **Carbohydrates:** 4g, **Sugar:** 2g, **Protein:** 22g, **Sodium:** 140mg, **Fiber:** 1g

STEAMED BROCCOLI & SCRAMBLED TOFU PLATE

INGREDIENTS

- 200g firm tofu, crumbled
- 1 cup broccoli florets
- ½ tsp turmeric powder
- ¼ tsp black pepper
- ½ tsp garlic powder
- 1 tbsp water

PREP TIME: 10 MINS

COOK TIME: 12 MINS

SERVING: 2

INSTRUCTIONS

1. Heat a non-stick skillet on moderate heat and toss in the crumbled tofu with 1 tbsp of water.
2. Sprinkle in turmeric, black pepper, and garlic powder, then stir well to coat.
3. Cook for 5-6 minutes, stirring at intervals, until the tofu turns a light golden color.
4. In a separate pot, steam the broccoli for 5 minutes.
5. Serve immediately, plating the scrambled tofu alongside the steamed broccoli.

Nutrition

Calories: 140, **Fat:** 4g, **Cholesterol:** 0mg, **Carbohydrates:** 5g, **Sugar:** 2g, **Protein:** 18g, **Sodium:** 130mg, **Fiber:** 2g

Storage & Reheating:

Refrigeration: Store in an airtight wide-mouth jar for up to 3 days.
Freezing: Not recommended.
Reheating: Microwave for 30-60 seconds or reheat on moderate heat in a skillet.

CAULIFLOWER RICE PORRIDGE WITH NONFAT YOGURT

INGREDIENTS

- 1 cup cauliflower rice
- ½ cup nonfat Greek yogurt (plain, unsweetened)
- ½ tsp cinnamon
- ½ tsp vanilla extract (optional)
- 1 tbsp water

PREP TIME: 5 MINS   **COOK TIME:** 10 MINS   **SERVING:** 2

INSTRUCTIONS

1. Heat a small saucepan on moderate heat and toss in the cauliflower rice with 1 tbsp of water.
2. Cook for 5-6 minutes, stirring with intervals, until the cauliflower softens and reaches a porridge-like consistency.
3. Remove and put it aside to cool slightly.
4. Stir in the nonfat Greek yogurt, cinnamon, and vanilla extract (if using).
5. Serve warm for a comforting, low-carb breakfast option.

Nutrition
Calories: 90, **Fat:** 1g, **Cholesterol:** 5mg, **Carbohydrates:** 5g, **Sugar:** 3g, **Protein:** 14g, **Sodium:** 60mg, **Fiber:** 2g

Storage & Reheating:

Refrigeration: Store in an airtight wide-mouth jar for up to 2 days.
Freezing: Not recommended.
Reheating: Microwave for 30-45 seconds, stirring halfway through.

LUNCH

GRILLED CHICKEN SALAD WITH LEMON VINAIGRETTE

INGREDIENTS

- 200g skinless chicken breast
- 4 cups mixed greens (lettuce, spinach, arugula)
- ½ cup cherry tomatoes, halved
- ½ cup cucumbers, sliced
- ½ tsp black pepper
- ½ tsp dried oregano
- 1 tbsp lemon juice
- 1 tsp apple cider vinegar
- 1 tbsp water

 PREP TIME: 10 MINS   **COOK TIME:** 15 MINS   **SERVING:** 2

INSTRUCTIONS

1. Preheat a grill pan on moderate heat and massage the chicken breast with black pepper and oregano.
2. Grill the chicken for 6-7 minutes on one side until fully cooked. Remove from the stove flame and let it rest for 2 minutes before slicing.
3. Take the small shallow bowl and whisk together lemon juice, apple cider vinegar, and water to create a light vinaigrette.
4. In a large, deep-bottom bowl, combine mixed greens, cherry tomatoes, and cucumbers.
5. Top with the grilled chicken slices, and drizzle the lemon vinaigrette over the salad.
6. Serve fresh, and enjoy!

Nutrition

Calories: 210, **Fat:** 3g, **Cholesterol:** 55mg, **Carbohydrates:** 7g, **Sugar:** 3g, **Protein:** 35g, **Sodium:** 170mg, **Fiber:** 3g

Storage & Reheating:

Refrigeration: Store salad and dressing separately in airtight containers for up to 2 days.

Freezing: Not recommended.

Reheating: Reheat the chicken using the microwave for 30-45 seconds if needed.

TURKEY LETTUCE WRAPS WITH MUSTARD

INGREDIENTS

- 150g lean ground turkey
- 4 large lettuce leaves (Romaine or Butterhead)
- ½ cup bell peppers, diced
- ½ cup onions, finely chopped
- 1 tbsp sugar-free mustard
- ½ tsp garlic powder
- ¼ tsp black pepper
- 1 tbsp water

 PREP TIME: 10 MINS   **COOK TIME:** 10 MINS   **SERVING:** 2

INSTRUCTIONS

1. Heat a non-stick skillet on moderate heat. Add the onions and bell peppers and 1 tbsp of water. Cook for 3-4 minutes until softened.
2. Add minced turkey and break it up with a spatula, stirring at intervals for 5-6 minutes until browned and fully cooked.
3. Stir in garlic powder, black pepper, and mustard, mixing well to coat the turkey evenly.
4. Spoon the mixture into the lettuce leaves, rolling them tightly into wraps.
5. Serve immediately and enjoy!

Nutrition

Calories: 180, **Fat:** 3g, **Cholesterol:** 40mg, **Carbohydrates:** 5g, **Sugar:** 2g, **Protein:** 28g, **Sodium:** 180mg, **Fiber:** 1g

Storage & Reheating:

Refrigeration: Store the turkey filling in an airtight container for up to 3 days.

Freezing: Not recommended.

Reheating: Microwave for 30-60 seconds before assembling the wraps.

CAULIFLOWER & LEAN CHICKEN STIR-FRY

INGREDIENTS

- 200g skinless chicken breast, diced
- 1 cup cauliflower rice
- ½ cup bell peppers, diced
- ½ cup onions, finely chopped
- ½ tsp garlic powder
- ¼ tsp black pepper
- ½ tsp dried basil
- 1 tbsp water

PREP TIME: 10 MINS **COOK TIME:** 15 MINS **SERVING:** 2

INSTRUCTIONS

1. Heat a non-stick skillet on moderate heat and toss in diced onions and bell peppers with 1 tbsp of water. Sauté for 3-4 minutes until softened.
2. Add diced meat and cook for 5-6 minutes, stirring at intervals, until browned and fully cooked.
3. Toss in the cauliflower rice, garlic powder, black pepper, and basil. Stir well to combine.
4. Cook for more than 5 minutes, stirring at intervals, until the cauliflower is tender and absorbs the flavors.
5. Serve immediately and enjoy!

Nutrition

Calories: 200, **Fat:** 3g, **Cholesterol:** 50mg, **Carbohydrates:** 7g, **Sugar:** 2g, **Protein:** 35g, **Sodium:** 180mg, **Fiber:** 2g

Storage & Reheating:

Refrigeration: Store in an airtight container for up to 3 days.
Freezing: Freeze for up to 2 months.
Reheating: Microwave for 1-2 minutes or reheat on moderate heat in a skillet.

SPICY EGG WHITE & MUSHROOM SCRAMBLE BOWL

INGREDIENTS

- 6 egg whites
- 1 cup mushrooms, sliced
- ½ cup onions, finely chopped
- ½ tsp chili powder
- ¼ tsp black pepper
- ½ tsp garlic powder
- 1 tbsp water

 PREP TIME: 10 MINS   **COOK TIME:** 10 MINS   **SERVING:** 2

INSTRUCTIONS

1. Heat a non-stick skillet on moderate heat and toss in the onions and mushrooms with 1 tbsp of water. Sauté for 3-4 minutes until softened.
2. Whisk the egg whites in a deep-bottom bowl with chili powder, black pepper, and garlic powder.
3. Ladle egg whites into the skillet, allowing them to set slightly.
4. Gently stir the eggs, breaking them into soft curds. Cook for more 2-3 minutes until fully set.
5. Serve warm; powder some extra chili powder on top if desired.

Nutrition

Calories: 120, **Fat:** 1g, **Cholesterol:** 0mg, **Carbohydrates:** 5g, **Sugar:** 2g, **Protein:** 22g, **Sodium:** 160mg, **Fiber:** 1g

Storage & Reheating:

Refrigeration: Store in an airtight container for up to 2 days.
Freezing: Not recommended.
Reheating: Microwave for 30-45 seconds or reheat on moderate heat in a skillet.

ZUCCHINI NOODLES WITH GARLIC & SHRIMP

INGREDIENTS

- 150g shrimp, peeled and deveined
- 2 cups zucchini noodles
- ½ cup bell peppers, sliced
- ½ tsp garlic powder
- ¼ tsp black pepper
- 1 tsp lemon juice
- 1 tbsp water

 PREP TIME: 15 MINS   **COOK TIME:** 10 MINS   **SERVING:** 2

INSTRUCTIONS

1. Heat a non-stick skillet on moderate heat. Toss in the shrimp with garlic powder and black pepper. Cook for 3-4 minutes, flipping halfway, until pink and cooked through.
2. Add the bell peppers and cook for more 2 minutes until slightly softened.
3. Toss in the zucchini noodles and water, stirring well. Cook for 2-3 minutes, just until the noodles soften slightly.
4. Drizzle with lemon juice before serving.

Nutrition
Calories: 160, **Fat:** 2g, **Cholesterol:** 120mg, **Carbohydrates:** 6g, **Sugar:** 2g, **Protein:** 28g, **Sodium:** 200mg, **Fiber:** 1g

Storage & Reheating:

Refrigeration: Store in an airtight container for up to 2 days.
Freezing: Not recommended.
Reheating: Microwave for 1 minute or reheat on moderate heat in a skillet.

BROCCOLI & TURKEY SOUP

INGREDIENTS

- 150g lean ground turkey
- 2 cups broccoli florets
- ½ cup onions, chopped
- 2 cups low-sodium chicken broth
- ½ tsp garlic powder
- ¼ tsp black pepper
- ½ tsp dried thyme

 PREP TIME: 10 MINS   **COOK TIME:** 20 MINS   **SERVING:** 2

INSTRUCTIONS

1. Heat a non-stick pot on moderate heat and toss in the onions. Cook for 2-3 minutes until softened.
2. Add minced meat, breaking it up with a spatula. Cook for 5-6 minutes, stirring at intervals, until browned.
3. Ladle in the chicken broth, then toss in the broccoli, garlic powder, black pepper, and thyme.
4. Get to a gentle simmer and cook for 10 minutes until the broccoli looks tender.
5. Serve hot and enjoy!

Nutrition

Calories: 170, **Fat:** 3g, **Cholesterol:** 40mg, **Carbohydrates:** 7g, **Sugar:** 3g, **Protein:** 28g, **Sodium:** 180mg, **Fiber:** 2g

Storage & Reheating:

Refrigeration: Store in an airtight for up to 3 days.
Freezing: Freeze for up to 2 months.
Reheating: Microwave for 1-2 minutes or reheat on moderate heat on the stovetop.

TUNA & CUCUMBER SALAD WITH MUSTARD DRESSING

INGREDIENTS

- 1 can tuna in water, drained
- 1 cup cucumbers, diced
- ½ cup cherry tomatoes, halved
- 1 tbsp sugar-free mustard
- ½ tsp black pepper
- ½ tsp dried dill
- 1 tsp lemon juice

PREP TIME: 5 MINS | **COOK TIME:** 00 MINS | **SERVING:** 2

INSTRUCTIONS

1. No cooking required. Grab the shallow bowl and combine the drained tuna, diced cucumbers, and cherry tomatoes.
2. Whisk together the mustard, black pepper, dill, and lemon juice.
3. Drizzle the lemon mustard dressing over the salad and gently toss to combine.
4. Serve immediately and enjoy fresh!

Nutrition

Calories: 140, **Fat:** 1g, **Cholesterol:** 40mg, **Carbohydrates:** 5g, **Sugar:** 2g, **Protein:** 26g, **Sodium:** 180mg, **Fiber:** 1g

Storage & Reheating:

Refrigeration: Store in an airtight container for up to 2 days.
Freezing: Not recommended.
Reheating: Not needed.

TURKEY & SPINACH STUFFED BELL PEPPERS

INGREDIENTS

- 2 large bell peppers, halved and deseeded
- 150g lean ground turkey
- 1 cup spinach, chopped
- ½ cup onions, diced
- ½ tsp garlic powder
- ¼ tsp black pepper
- ½ tsp dried oregano

PREP TIME: 10 MINS

COOK TIME: 25 MINS

SERVING: 2

INSTRUCTIONS

1. Preheat oven to 375°F (190°C).
2. Heat a non-stick skillet on moderate heat and toss in the onions. Sauté for 2-3 minutes until softened.
3. Add minced turkey, breaking it up with a spatula. Cook for 5-6 minutes until browned.
4. Stir in the spinach, garlic powder, black pepper, and oregano. Cook for more than 2 minutes until the spinach wilts.
5. Spoon the meat mixture into the bell pepper halves and shift them to the baking dish.
6. Bake for 15 minutes until the peppers soften.
7. Serve warm and enjoy!

Nutrition
Calories: 190, **Fat:** 3g, **Cholesterol:** 40mg, **Carbohydrates:** 8g, **Sugar:** 3g, **Protein:** 30g, **Sodium:** 160mg, **Fiber:** 2g

Storage & Reheating:

Refrigeration: Store in an airtight container for up to 3 days.

Freezing: Freeze for up to 2 months.

Reheating: Microwave for 1-2 minutes or reheat on moderate heat in the oven.

GRILLED FISH WITH LEMON & STEAMED VEGGIES

INGREDIENTS

- 200g white fish fillet (tilapia, cod, or flounder)
- 1 cup broccoli florets
- 1 cup zucchini slices
- ½ tsp garlic powder
- ¼ tsp black pepper
- 1 tsp lemon juice
- 1 tbsp water

 PREP TIME: 10 MINS   **COOK TIME:** 15 MINS   **SERVING:** 2

INSTRUCTIONS

1. Preheat a grill pan on moderate heat and massage the fish with garlic powder, black pepper, and lemon juice.
2. Grill the fish for 4-5 minutes on one side until golden and fully cooked.
3. Meanwhile, steam the broccoli and zucchini in a pot with 1 tbsp water for 5 minutes, until tender but slightly crisp.
4. Plate the fish with the steamed veggies on the side and serve warm.

Nutrition

Calories: 170, **Fat:** 2g, **Cholesterol:** 50mg, **Carbohydrates:** 6g, **Sugar:** 2g, **Protein:** 30g, **Sodium:** 180mg, **Fiber:** 2g

Storage & Reheating:

Refrigeration: Store in an airtight container for up to 2 days.
Freezing: Freeze for up to 2 months.
Reheating: Microwave for 1-2 minutes or reheat on moderate heat in a skillet.

CABBAGE SLAW WITH GRILLED CHICKEN STRIPS

INGREDIENTS

- 200g skinless chicken breast
- 2 cups shredded cabbage
- ½ cup carrots, julienned
- ½ tsp garlic powder
- ¼ tsp black pepper
- 1 tbsp apple cider vinegar
- 1 tsp lemon juice

PREP TIME: 10 MINS

COOK TIME: 15 MINS

SERVING: 2

INSTRUCTIONS

1. Preheat a grill pan on moderate heat and massage the chicken breast with garlic powder and black pepper.
2. Grill the chicken for 6-7 minutes on one side until golden brown and fully cooked. Let it rest for 2 minutes before slicing into strips.
3. Take the large shallow bowl and combine the cabbage and carrots.
4. Drizzle with apple cider vinegar and lemon juice, then toss well to coat evenly.
5. Top with the grilled chicken strips and serve fresh.

Nutrition

Calories: 190, **Fat:** 3g, **Cholesterol:** 50mg, **Carbohydrates:** 8g, **Sugar:** 4g, **Protein:** 30g, **Sodium:** 170mg, **Fiber:** 3g

Storage & Reheating:

Refrigeration: Store salad and chicken separately in airtight containers for up to 2 days.

Freezing: Not recommended.

Reheating: Microwave the chicken for 30-45 seconds if needed.

MUSHROOM & TOFU STIR-FRY WITH GARLIC

INGREDIENTS

- 200g firm tofu, cut into small cubes
- 1 cup mushrooms, sliced
- ½ cup bell peppers, diced
- ½ tsp garlic powder
- ¼ tsp black pepper
- ½ tsp dried basil
- 1 tbsp water

PREP TIME: 10 MINS	COOK TIME: 12 MINS	SERVING: 2

INSTRUCTIONS

1. Heat a non-stick skillet on moderate heat and toss in the tofu cubes. Let them cook for 3-4 minutes, flipping occasionally, until slightly golden.
2. Add the mushrooms and bell peppers along with 1 tbsp of water. Stir-fry for 4-5 minutes until softened.
3. Sprinkle in garlic powder, crushed pepper, and dried basil. Stir well to coat the ingredients evenly.
4. Cook for more than 2 minutes, allowing the flavors to blend.
5. Serve immediately and enjoy!

Nutrition
Calories: 150, **Fat:** 4g, **Cholesterol:** 0mg, **Carbohydrates:** 6g, **Sugar:** 2g, **Protein:** 18g, **Sodium:** 130mg, **Fiber:** 2g

Storage & Reheating:

Refrigeration: Store in an airtight container large-size jar for up to 3 days.

Freezing: Not recommended.

Reheating: Microwave for 30-60 seconds or reheat on moderate heat in a skillet.

LEMON HERB TURKEY SKEWERS WITH ZUCCHINI

INGREDIENTS

- 200g skinless turkey breast, cubed
- 1 cup zucchini, sliced into rounds
- ½ tsp garlic powder
- ¼ tsp black pepper
- ½ tsp dried oregano
- 1 tsp lemon juice

PREP TIME: 15 MINS
COOK TIME: 15 MINS
SERVING: 2

INSTRUCTIONS

1. Grab the shallow bowl and massage the turkey cubes with garlic powder, black pepper, oregano, and lemon juice. Put them aside to sit for 5 minutes to absorb the flavors.
2. Thread the turkey and zucchini onto skewers, alternating between them.
3. Preheat a grill pan on moderate heat and place the skewers on the pan.
4. Cook for 4-5 minutes on one side, turning occasionally until the turkey is golden brown and fully cooked.
5. Serve immediately and enjoy!

Nutrition
Calories: 180, **Fat:** 3g, **Cholesterol:** 45mg, **Carbohydrates:** 5g, **Sugar:** 2g, **Protein:** 32g, **Sodium:** 180mg, **Fiber:** 1g

Storage & Reheating:

Refrigeration: Store in an airtight container large-size jar for up to 2 days.

Freezing: Not recommended.

Reheating: Microwave for 1 minute or reheat on moderate heat in a skillet.

STEAMED TILAPIA WITH SPINACH & VINEGAR DRESSING

INGREDIENTS

- 200g tilapia fillet
- 1 cup fresh spinach
- ½ tsp garlic powder
- ¼ tsp black pepper
- 1 tbsp apple cider vinegar
- 1 tbsp water

PREP TIME: 10 MINS

COOK TIME: 15 MINS

SERVING: 2

INSTRUCTIONS

1. In a steamer, place the raw tilapia fillet over a layer of spinach.
2. Sprinkle ground garlic and black pepper over the fish.
3. Steam for 10-12 minutes until the tilapia gets opaque and flakes easily.
4. Drizzle apple cider vinegar over the fish and spinach before serving.

Nutrition
Calories: 160, **Fat:** 2g, **Cholesterol:** 50mg, **Carbohydrates:** 4g, **Sugar:** 1g, **Protein:** 32g, **Sodium:** 170mg, **Fiber:** 1g

Storage & Reheating:

Refrigeration: Store in an airtight container large-size jar for up to 2 days.

Freezing: Not recommended.

Reheating: Microwave for 1-2 minutes.

CAULIFLOWER RICE SUSHI WITH LEAN TUNA

INGREDIENTS

- 1 cup raw cauliflower, finely grated
- 100g fresh raw tuna, thinly sliced
- ½ small cucumber, julienned
- ½ tsp black pepper
- ½ tsp dried seaweed flakes (optional)

 PREP TIME: 15 MINS   **COOK TIME:** 5 MINS   **SERVING:** 2

INSTRUCTIONS

1. Place the grated cauliflower in a dry, non-stick pan and cook for 5 minutes on moderate heat, stirring at intervals until slightly soft. Let cool.
2. Spread the cauliflower "rice" on a piece of plastic wrap, forming a rectangle.
3. Layer the fresh tuna slices and cucumber along one edge of the cauliflower.
4. Roll tightly with the help of plastic wrap to form a sushi roll.
5. Slice into bite-sized pieces, sprinkle with black pepper and optional seaweed flakes and serve.

Nutrition

Calories: 140, **Fat:** 2g, **Cholesterol:** 40mg, **Carbohydrates:** 5g, **Sugar:** 1g, **Protein:** 28g, **Sodium:** 180mg, **Fiber:** 1g

Storage & Reheating:

Refrigeration: Store in an airtight container large-size jar for up to 1 day.

Freezing: Not recommended.

Reheating: Not needed.

ZESTY GRILLED SHRIMP WITH CABBAGE SLAW

INGREDIENTS

- 150g raw shrimp, peeled and deveined
- 1 cup shredded cabbage
- ½ cup carrots, julienned
- ½ tsp garlic powder
- ¼ tsp black pepper
- 1 tsp lemon juice
- 1 tbsp apple cider vinegar

PREP TIME: 10 MINS **COOK TIME:** 10 MINS **SERVING:** 2

INSTRUCTIONS

1. Grab the shallow bowl and massage the shrimp with ground powder, black pepper, and lemon juice. Let sit for 5 minutes.
2. Preheat a grill pan on moderate heat. Grill the shrimp for 3-4 minutes on one side until pink and fully cooked.
3. Take the large shallow bowl and combine the shredded cabbage and carrots.
4. Drizzle with apple cider vinegar and toss well to coat evenly.
5. Top with the grilled shrimp and serve immediately.

Nutrition
Calories: 160, **Fat:** 2g, **Cholesterol:** 120mg, **Carbohydrates:** 6g, **Sugar:** 2g, **Protein:** 28g, **Sodium:** 200mg, **Fiber:** 1g

Storage & Reheating:

Refrigeration: Store salad and shrimp separately in airtight containers for up to 2 days.

Freezing: Not recommended.

Reheating: Microwave the shrimp for 30-45 seconds before serving.

LOW-CARB GREEK CHICKEN SALAD

INGREDIENTS

- 200g skinless chicken breast
- 2 cups mixed greens (lettuce, spinach, arugula)
- ½ cup cucumbers, sliced
- ½ cup cherry tomatoes, halved
- ¼ cup nonfat Greek yogurt (or unsweetened coconut yogurt for dairy-free)
- ½ tsp garlic powder
- ½ tsp dried oregano
- ¼ tsp black pepper
- 1 tbsp lemon juice

PREP TIME: 10 MINS
COOK TIME: 15 MINS
SERVING: 2

INSTRUCTIONS

1. Massage the chicken breast with garlic powder, oregano, and black pepper. Let it sit for 5 minutes.
2. Heat a non-stick skillet on moderate heat. Grill the chicken for 6-7 minutes on one side until golden and fully cooked. Let it rest for 2 minutes, then slice.
3. Take the large shallow bowl and toss in the mixed greens, cucumbers, and cherry tomatoes.
4. Take the small shallow bowl and whisk together Greek yogurt with lemon juice to create a dressing.
5. Spread grilled chicken slices on top and drizzle the dressing over it before serving.

Nutrition

Calories: 200, **Fat:** 3g, **Cholesterol:** 50mg, **Carbohydrates:** 8g, **Sugar:** 3g, **Protein:** 34g, **Sodium:** 180mg, **Fiber:** 2g

Storage & Reheating:

Refrigeration: Store salad and dressing separately in airtight containers for up to 2 days.

Freezing: Not recommended.

Reheating: Reheat chicken in a skillet or microwave for 30-45 seconds before serving.

GRILLED CHICKEN & CUCUMBER LETTUCE WRAPS

INGREDIENTS

- 200g skinless chicken breast, diced
- 4 large lettuce leaves (Romaine or Butterhead)
- ½ cup cucumbers, julienned
- ½ tsp garlic powder
- ¼ tsp black pepper
- ½ tsp dried dill
- 1 tbsp lemon juice

PREP TIME: 10 MINS	**COOK TIME:** 12 MINS	**SERVING:** 2

INSTRUCTIONS

1. Massage the diced chicken with garlic powder, black pepper, and dill. Let it sit for 5 minutes.
2. Heat a non-stick skillet on moderate heat. Grill the chicken for 5-6 minutes, stirring at intervals, until golden and fully cooked.
3. Spread the lettuce leaves and divide the cucumbers evenly among them.
4. Spoon in the grilled chicken and drizzle with lemon juice before rolling into wraps.
5. Serve immediately and enjoy fresh!

Nutrition

Calories: 180, **Fat:** 2g, **Cholesterol:** 40mg, **Carbohydrates:** 6g, **Sugar:** 2g, **Protein:** 30g, **Sodium:** 160mg, **Fiber:** 1g

Storage & Reheating:

Refrigeration: Store chicken and lettuce separately in airtight containers for up to 2 days.

Freezing: Not recommended.

Reheating: Reheat chicken in the microwave for 30-45 seconds before assembling wraps.

STEAMED SHRIMP WITH ZUCCHINI & GARLIC SAUCE

INGREDIENTS

- 150g raw shrimp, peeled and deveined
- 1 cup zucchini, sliced
- ½ tsp garlic powder
- ¼ tsp black pepper
- 1 tsp lemon juice
- 1 tbsp apple cider vinegar

PREP TIME: 10 MINS

COOK TIME: 10 MINS

SERVING: 2

INSTRUCTIONS

1. Grab the shallow bowl and massage the shrimp with ground garlic, black pepper, and lemon juice. Let sit for 5 minutes.
2. Place the shrimp and zucchini slices in a steamer. Steam for 7-8 minutes, or until the shrimp turns pink and the zucchini is tender.
3. Drizzle with apple cider vinegar before serving.

Nutrition

Calories: 160, **Fat:** 2g, **Cholesterol:** 120mg, **Carbohydrates:** 5g, **Sugar:** 2g, **Protein:** 28g, **Sodium:** 180mg, **Fiber:** 1g

Storage & Reheating:

Refrigeration: Store in an airtight container large-size jar for up to 2 days.

Freezing: Not recommended.

Reheating: Microwave for 30-45 seconds.

GRILLED TILAPIA WITH SPINACH & LEMON DRESSING

INGREDIENTS

- 200g tilapia fillet
- 1 cup spinach, chopped
- ½ tsp garlic powder
- ¼ tsp black pepper
- 1 tbsp lemon juice
- 1 tbsp water

 PREP TIME: 10 MINS   **COOK TIME:** 12 MINS   **SERVING:** 2

INSTRUCTIONS

1. Massage the tilapia fillet with garlic powder and black pepper. Let it sit for 5 minutes.
2. Preheat a grill pan on moderate heat. Grill the tilapia for 4-5 minutes on one side until golden and flaky.
3. In a skillet, toss in the spinach with 1 tbsp water and sauté for 2 minutes until wilted.
4. Plate the fish over the spinach and drizzle with lemon juice before serving.

Nutrition
Calories: 170, **Fat:** 3g, **Cholesterol:** 50mg, **Carbohydrates:** 5g, **Sugar:** 2g, **Protein:** 32g, **Sodium:** 170mg, **Fiber:** 1g

Storage & Reheating:

Refrigeration: Store in an airtight container large-size jar for up to 2 days.

Freezing: Not recommended.

Reheating: Microwave for 1-2 minutes.

SPICY GROUND TURKEY & BROCCOLI BOWL

INGREDIENTS

- 150g lean ground turkey
- 1 cup broccoli florets
- ½ tsp chili powder
- ¼ tsp black pepper
- ½ tsp garlic powder
- 1 tbsp water

PREP TIME: 10 MINS   **COOK TIME:** 15 MINS   **SERVING:** 2

INSTRUCTIONS

1. Heat a non-stick skillet on moderate heat and toss in the ground turkey. Cook for 5-6 minutes, breaking it apart as it browns.
2. Add the broccoli and 1 tbsp water. Cook for more than 5 minutes, stirring at intervals.
3. Sprinkle with chili powder, black pepper, and garlic powder, stirring well to coat.
4. Cook more for 2 minutes, then serve hot.

Nutrition

Calories: 190, **Fat:** 3g, **Cholesterol:** 45mg, **Carbohydrates:** 7g, **Sugar:** 2g, **Protein:** 32g, **Sodium:** 170mg, **Fiber:** 2g

Storage & Reheating:

Refrigeration: Store in an airtight container large-size jar for up to 3 days.

Freezing: Freeze for up to 2 months.

Reheating: Microwave for 1-2 minutes or reheat on moderate heat in a skillet.

DINNER

LEMON GARLIC BAKED COD WITH BROCCOLI

INGREDIENTS

- 200g cod fillet
- 2 cups broccoli florets
- 1 tbsp lemon juice
- ½ tsp garlic powder
- ¼ tsp black pepper
- ½ tsp dried oregano
- 1 tbsp water

PREP TIME: 10 MINS

COOK TIME: 15 MINS

SERVING: 2

INSTRUCTIONS

1. Preheat oven to 375°F (190°C).
2. Massage the cod fillet with lemon juice, garlic powder, black pepper, and oregano.
3. Place cod in a baking dish and add 1 tbsp water to prevent drying.
4. Bake for 12-15 minutes until the fillet flakes easily.
5. Meanwhile, steam the broccoli in a pot with 1 tbsp water for 5 minutes until tender but slightly crisp.
6. Serve immediately with steamed broccoli on the side.

Nutrition
Calories: 180, **Fat:** 2g, **Cholesterol:** 50mg, **Carbohydrates:** 6g, **Sugar:** 2g, **Protein:** 34g, **Sodium:** 170mg, **Fiber:** 3g

Storage & Reheating:

Refrigeration: Store in an airtight container large-size jar for up to 2 days.

Freezing: Not recommended.

Reheating: Microwave for 1-2 minutes or reheat on moderate heat in a skillet.

ROASTED TILAPIA WITH CABBAGE & HERB DRESSING

INGREDIENTS

- 200g tilapia fillet
- 1 cup cabbage, shredded
- ½ tsp garlic powder
- ¼ tsp black pepper
- ½ tsp dried basil
- 1 tbsp lemon juice
- 1 tbsp water

PREP TIME: 10 MINS **COOK TIME:** 15 MINS **SERVING:** 2

INSTRUCTIONS

1. Preheat oven to 375°F (190°C).
2. Massage the tilapia fillet with garlic powder, black pepper, basil, and lemon juice.
3. Place fish on a baking sheet arranged with parchment paper.
4. Roast for 12-15 minutes until the fish turns golden and flakes easily.
5. Meanwhile, in a skillet, toss in the shredded cabbage with 1 tbsp water and sauté for 2-3 minutes until slightly tender.
6. Plate the roasted tilapia over the cabbage and serve warm.

Nutrition

Calories: 170, **Fat:** 2g, **Cholesterol:** 50mg, **Carbohydrates:** 5g, **Sugar:** 1g, **Protein:** 32g, **Sodium:** 160mg, **Fiber:** 2g

Storage & Reheating:

Refrigeration: Store in an airtight container large-size jar for up to 2 days.

Freezing: Not recommended.

Reheating: Microwave for 1-2 minutes or reheat on moderate heat in a skillet.

LOW-CARB TURKEY & CABBAGE SLAW STIR-FRY

INGREDIENTS

- 150g lean ground turkey
- 1 cup cabbage, shredded
- ½ cup bell peppers, diced
- ½ tsp garlic powder
- ¼ tsp black pepper
- ½ tsp dried thyme
- 1 tbsp water

PREP TIME: 15 MINS   **COOK TIME:** 15 MINS   **SERVING:** 2

INSTRUCTIONS

1. Heat a non-stick skillet on moderate heat and toss in the ground turkey. Cook for 5-6 minutes, breaking it apart as it browns.
2. Add cabbage, bell peppers, and 1 tbsp water. Stir well and cook for more 5 minutes until softened.
3. Sprinkle with garlic powder, black pepper, and thyme, mixing well.
4. Cook more for 2 minutes, ensuring the flavors blend well.
5. Serve warm and enjoy!

Nutrition
Calories: 190, **Fat:** 3g, **Cholesterol:** 45mg, **Carbohydrates:** 7g, **Sugar:** 2g, **Protein:** 32g, **Sodium:** 170mg, **Fiber:** 2g

Storage & Reheating:

Refrigeration: Store in an airtight container large-size jar for up to 3 days.

Freezing: Freeze for up to 2 months.

Reheating: Microwave for 1-2 minutes or reheat on moderate heat in a skillet.

LEAN CHICKEN STIR-FRY WITH BOK CHOY

INGREDIENTS

- 200g skinless chicken breast, diced
- 1 cup bok choy, chopped
- ½ cup mushrooms, sliced
- ½ tsp garlic powder
- ¼ tsp black pepper
- ½ tsp dried basil
- 1 tbsp water

PREP TIME: 10 MINS **COOK TIME:** 12 MINS **SERVING:** 2

INSTRUCTIONS

1. Heat a non-stick skillet on moderate heat. Add the diced chicken and stir-fry for 5-6 minutes, until lightly golden.
2. Add the bok choy, mushrooms, and 1 tbsp water. Cook for 5 more minutes, stirring with intervals.
3. Sprinkle with garlic powder, black pepper, and basil, mixing well.
4. Cook for more than 2 minutes, allowing flavors to blend.
5. Serve immediately and enjoy!

Nutrition

Calories: 180, **Fat:** 2g, **Cholesterol:** 50mg, **Carbohydrates:** 6g, **Sugar:** 2g, **Protein:** 34g, **Sodium:** 160mg, **Fiber:** 2g

Storage & Reheating:

Refrigeration: Store in an airtight container large-size jar for up to 3 days.

Freezing: Freeze for up to 2 months.

Reheating: Microwave for 1-2 minutes or reheat on moderate heat in a skillet.

GRILLED TURKEY & MUSHROOM SKEWERS

INGREDIENTS

- 200g skinless turkey breast, cubed
- 1 cup mushrooms, whole or halved
- ½ tsp garlic powder
- ¼ tsp black pepper
- ½ tsp dried oregano
- 1 tsp lemon juice

PREP TIME: 10 MINS   **COOK TIME:** 15 MINS   **SERVING:** 2

INSTRUCTIONS

1. Grab the shallow bowl and massage the turkey cubes with garlic powder, black pepper, oregano, and lemon juice. Let sit for 5 minutes.
2. Thread the turkey and mushrooms onto skewers, alternating between them.
3. Preheat a grill pan on moderate heat. Grill the skewers for 4-5 minutes on one side, until golden and fully cooked.
4. Serve warm and enjoy!

Nutrition

Calories: 190, **Fat:** 3g, **Cholesterol:** 50mg, **Carbohydrates:** 5g, **Sugar:** 2g, **Protein:** 32g, **Sodium:** 180mg, **Fiber:** 1g

Storage & Reheating:

Refrigeration: Store in an airtight container large-size jar for up to 2 days.

Freezing: Not recommended.

Reheating: Microwave for 1-2 minutes or reheat on moderate heat in a skillet.

BAKED LEMON CHICKEN WITH CAULIFLOWER RICE

INGREDIENTS

- 200g skinless chicken breast
- 1 cup cauliflower rice
- 1 tbsp lemon juice
- ½ tsp garlic powder
- ½ tsp dried oregano
- ¼ tsp black pepper
- 1 tbsp water

PREP TIME: 10 MINS   **COOK TIME:** 20 MINS   **SERVING:** 2

INSTRUCTIONS

1. Preheat oven to 375°F (190°C).
2. Massage the chicken breast with lemon juice, garlic powder, oregano, and black pepper.
3. Place chicken in a baking dish, adding 1 tbsp water to prevent drying.
4. Bake for 18-20 minutes or until the chicken is fully cooked.
5. Meanwhile, heat a non-stick skillet on moderate heat and toss in the cauliflower rice. Cook for 5 minutes, stirring at intervals, until tender.
6. Serve the baked lemon chicken over cauliflower rice, and enjoy!

Nutrition

Calories: 200, **Fat:** 3g, **Cholesterol:** 50mg, **Carbohydrates:** 7g, **Sugar:** 2g, **Protein:** 34g, **Sodium:** 170mg, **Fiber:** 2g

Storage & Reheating:

Refrigeration: Store in an airtight container large-size jar for up to 3 days.

Freezing: Freeze for up to 2 months.

Reheating: Microwave for 1-2 minutes or reheat on moderate heat in a skillet.

SPAGHETTI SQUASH & SHRIMP BOWL

INGREDIENTS

- 150g raw shrimp, peeled and deveined
- 1 small spaghetti squash
- ½ tsp garlic powder
- ¼ tsp black pepper
- ½ tsp dried basil
- 1 tsp lemon juice
- 1 tbsp water

PREP TIME: 10 MINS

COOK TIME: 25 MINS

SERVING: 2

INSTRUCTIONS

1. Preheat oven to 375°F (190°C).
2. Cut the spaghetti squash in half to discard the seeds, and place face-down on the paper-arranged baking sheet. Bake for 20 minutes until soft.
3. Meanwhile, in a deep-bottom bowl, massage the shrimp with garlic powder, black pepper, and basil. Let it sit for 5 minutes.
4. Heat a non-stick skillet on moderate heat. Add the shrimp and 1 tbsp water. Cook for 3-4 minutes on one side until pink and fully cooked.
5. Scrape the spaghetti squash to produce the "noodles" and top with the cooked shrimp.
6. Drizzle with lemon juice and serve warm.

Nutrition
Calories: 180, **Fat:** 2g, **Cholesterol:** 120mg, **Carbohydrates:** 9g, **Sugar:** 4g, **Protein:** 30g, **Sodium:** 180mg, **Fiber:** 3g

Storage & Reheating:

Refrigeration: Store in an airtight container large-size jar for up to 2 days.

Freezing: Not recommended.

Reheating: Microwave for 1-2 minutes.

STEAMED FISH WITH ASPARAGUS & VINEGAR DRESSING

INGREDIENTS

- 200g white fish fillet (tilapia or cod)
- 1 cup asparagus, trimmed
- ½ tsp garlic powder
- ¼ tsp black pepper
- 1 tbsp apple cider vinegar
- 1 tbsp water

PREP TIME: 10 MINS   **COOK TIME:** 12 MINS   **SERVING:** 2

INSTRUCTIONS

1. In a steamer, place the fish fillet over the asparagus.
2. Sprinkle with garlic powder and black pepper.
3. Steam for 10-12 minutes until the fish gets opaque and flakes easily.
4. Drizzle with apple cider vinegar before serving.

Nutrition
Calories: 170, **Fat:** 2g, **Cholesterol:** 50mg, **Carbohydrates:** 5g, **Sugar:** 1g, **Protein:** 32g, **Sodium:** 160mg, **Fiber:** 2g

Storage & Reheating:

Refrigeration: Store in an airtight container for up to 2 days.
Freezing: Not recommended.
Reheating: Microwave for 1-2 minutes.

GARLIC & HERB TURKEY MEATBALLS

INGREDIENTS

- 150g lean ground turkey
- ½ cup cauliflower rice
- ½ tsp garlic powder
- ¼ tsp black pepper
- ½ tsp dried oregano
- 1 tbsp water

PREP TIME: 10 MINS

COOK TIME: 15 MINS

SERVING: 2

INSTRUCTIONS

1. Preheat oven to 375°F (190°C).
2. Grab the shallow bowl and combine ground turkey, cauliflower rice, garlic powder, black pepper, and oregano. Mix well.
3. Form small meatballs and place them on the paper-arranged baking sheet.
4. Bake for 12-15 minutes until fully cooked.
5. Serve warm and enjoy!

Nutrition
Calories: 180, **Fat:** 2g, **Cholesterol:** 45mg, **Carbohydrates:** 5g, **Sugar:** 2g, **Protein:** 32g, **Sodium:** 180mg, **Fiber:** 1g

Storage & Reheating:

Refrigeration: Store in an airtight container for up to 3 days.

Freezing: Freeze for up to 2 months.

Reheating: Microwave for 1-2 minutes or reheat on moderate heat in a skillet.

BAKED TURKEY & ZUCCHINI MEATLOAF

INGREDIENTS

- 150g lean ground turkey
- ½ cup zucchini, grated
- ½ tsp garlic powder
- ¼ tsp black pepper
- ½ tsp dried basil
- 1 tbsp water

 PREP TIME: 10 MINS   **COOK TIME:** 25 MINS   **SERVING:** 2

INSTRUCTIONS

1. Preheat oven to 375°F (190°C).
2. Grab the shallow bowl and combine ground turkey, grated zucchini, garlic powder, black pepper, and basil. Mix well.
3. Shape into a small meatloaf and place in a baking dish.
4. Bake for 20-25 minutes until fully cooked.
5. Serve warm and enjoy!

Nutrition
Calories: 190, **Fat:** 3g, **Cholesterol:** 50mg, **Carbohydrates:** 6g, **Sugar:** 2g, **Protein:** 32g, **Sodium:** 170mg, **Fiber:** 1g

Storage & Reheating:

Refrigeration: Store in an airtight container for up to 3 days.

Freezing: Freeze for up to 2 months.

Reheating: Microwave for 1-2 minutes or reheat on moderate heat in a skillet.

NONFAT COTTAGE CHEESE & CUCUMBER PROTEIN PLATE

INGREDIENTS

- 1 cup nonfat cottage cheese (or unsweetened coconut yogurt for dairy-free)
- 1 cup cucumbers, sliced
- ½ cup cherry tomatoes, halved
- ¼ tsp black pepper
- ½ tsp dried dill
- 1 tsp lemon juice

PREP TIME: 5 MINS **COOK TIME:** 00 MINS **SERVING:** 2

INSTRUCTIONS

1. Arrange the sliced cucumbers and cherry tomatoes on a plate.
2. Spoon the cottage cheese onto the plate and sprinkle with black pepper and dill.
3. Drizzle with lemon juice and serve fresh.

Nutrition
Calories: 140, **Fat:** 1g, **Cholesterol:** 10mg, **Carbohydrates:** 7g, **Sugar:** 4g, **Protein:** 24g, **Sodium:** 180mg, **Fiber:** 1g

Storage & Reheating:

Refrigeration: Store in an airtight container for up to 2 days.
Freezing: Not recommended.
Reheating: Not needed.

LEAN CHICKEN & CABBAGE SPRING ROLLS

INGREDIENTS

- 200g skinless chicken breast, sliced thin
- 4 large lettuce leaves (Romaine or Butterhead)
- 1 cup cabbage, shredded
- ½ tsp garlic powder
- ¼ tsp black pepper
- ½ tsp dried basil
- 1 tsp apple cider vinegar

PREP TIME: 15 MINS **COOK TIME:** 10 MINS **SERVING:** 2

INSTRUCTIONS

1. Massage the chicken slices with garlic powder, black pepper, and basil. Let it sit for 5 minutes.
2. Heat a non-stick skillet on moderate heat. Grill the breast meat for 4-5 minutes on one side until golden brown and fully cooked. Let it rest for 2 minutes, then slice it into thin strips.
3. Grab the shallow bowl and toss in the shredded cabbage with apple cider vinegar.
4. Spread the lettuce leaves and fill each with cabbage and sliced chicken.
5. Roll tightly into spring rolls and serve fresh.

Nutrition
Calories: 180, **Fat:** 2g, **Cholesterol:** 40mg, **Carbohydrates:** 6g, **Sugar:** 2g, **Protein:** 32g, **Sodium:** 160mg, **Fiber:** 2g

Storage & Reheating:

Refrigeration: Store lettuce and chicken separately in airtight containers for up to 2 days.

Freezing: Not recommended.

Reheating: Reheat chicken in a skillet or microwave for 30-45 seconds before assembling.

ROASTED SALMON WITH LEMON & ZUCCHINI

INGREDIENTS

- 200g salmon fillet
- 1 cup zucchini, sliced
- 1 tbsp lemon juice
- ½ tsp garlic powder
- ¼ tsp black pepper
- ½ tsp dried oregano
- 1 tbsp water

PREP TIME: 10 MINS

COOK TIME: 15 MINS

SERVING: 2

INSTRUCTIONS

1. Preheat oven to 375°F (190°C).
2. Massage the salmon fillet with lemon juice, garlic powder, black pepper, and oregano.
3. Place the salmon and zucchini slices on a baking sheet arranged with parchment paper.
4. Roast for 12-15 minutes until the salmon looks fully cooked.
5. Serve warm with roasted zucchini on the side.

Nutrition
Calories: 220, **Fat:** 8g, **Cholesterol:** 55mg, **Carbohydrates:** 5g, **Sugar:** 2g, **Protein:** 34g, **Sodium:** 180mg, **Fiber:** 1g

Storage & Reheating:

Refrigeration: Store in an airtight container for up to 2 days.
Freezing: Not recommended.
Reheating: Microwave for 1-2 minutes or reheat on moderate heat in a skillet.

CABBAGE STIR-FRY WITH GARLIC SHRIMP

INGREDIENTS

- 150g raw shrimp, peeled and deveined
- 1 cup cabbage, shredded
- ½ tsp garlic powder
- ¼ tsp black pepper
- ½ tsp dried thyme
- 1 tbsp apple cider vinegar
- 1 tbsp water

 PREP TIME: 10 MINS   **COOK TIME:** 10 MINS   **SERVING:** 2

INSTRUCTIONS

1. Grab the shallow bowl and massage the shrimp with garlic powder, black pepper, and thyme. Let sit for 5 minutes.
2. Heat a non-stick skillet on moderate heat and toss in the shrimp. Cook for 3-4 minutes on one side until pink and fully cooked. Remove and set aside.
3. In the same skillet, toss in the shredded cabbage and add 1 tbsp water. Cook for 5 minutes, stirring at intervals, until softened.
4. Drizzle with apple cider vinegar, stir well, and serve with shrimp on top.

Nutrition
Calories: 160, **Fat:** 2g, **Cholesterol:** 120mg, **Carbohydrates:** 6g, **Sugar:** 2g, **Protein:** 28g, **Sodium:** 180mg, **Fiber:** 1g

Storage & Reheating:

Refrigeration: Store shrimp and cabbage separately in airtight containers for up to 2 days.

Freezing: Not recommended.

Reheating: Microwave shrimp for 30-45 seconds before serving.

LOW-CARB GROUND TURKEY LETTUCE TACOS

INGREDIENTS

- 150g lean ground turkey
- 4 large lettuce leaves (Romaine or Butterhead)
- ½ cup cucumbers, diced
- ½ tsp garlic powder
- ¼ tsp black pepper
- ½ tsp dried oregano
- 1 tbsp lemon juice

PREP TIME: 10 MINS

COOK TIME: 12 MINS

SERVING: 2

INSTRUCTIONS

1. Heat a non-stick skillet on moderate heat and toss in the ground turkey. Cook for 5-6 minutes, breaking it apart as it browns.
2. Sprinkle with garlic powder, black pepper, and oregano, stirring well.
3. Cook for more 2 minutes, then remove form the stove flame and drizzle with lemon juice.
4. Spread the lettuce leaves and divide the turkey filling evenly among them.
5. Top with diced cucumbers and serve immediately.

Nutrition
Calories: 180, **Fat:** 2g, **Cholesterol:** 45mg, **Carbohydrates:** 6g, **Sugar:** 2g, **Protein:** 32g, **Sodium:** 160mg, **Fiber:** 2g

Storage & Reheating:

Refrigeration: Store lettuce and turkey separately in airtight containers for up to 2 days.

Freezing: Not recommended.

Reheating: Microwave turkey for 30-45 seconds before assembling tacos.

OVEN-BAKED FISH WITH GARLIC & HERBS

INGREDIENTS

- 200g white fish fillet (tilapia or cod)
- ½ tsp garlic powder
- ¼ tsp black pepper
- ½ tsp dried oregano
- 1 tbsp lemon juice
- 1 tbsp water

PREP TIME: 10 MINS **COOK TIME:** 15 MINS **SERVING:** 2

INSTRUCTIONS

1. Preheat oven to 375°F (190°C).
2. Massage the fish fillet with garlic powder, black pepper, oregano, and lemon juice.
3. Place the fillet in a baking dish. You may add 1 tablespoon of water to the dish to help prevent the fish from drying out while baking—this step is optional.
4. Bake for 12–15 minutes, or until the fish is fully cooked and flakes easily with a fork.
5. Serve warm and enjoy!

Nutrition
Calories: 170, **Fat:** 2g, **Cholesterol:** 50mg, **Carbohydrates:** 3g, **Sugar:** 1g, **Protein:** 32g, **Sodium:** 160mg, **Fiber:** 1g

Storage & Reheating:

Refrigeration: Store in an airtight container for up to 2 days.
Freezing: Not recommended.
Reheating: Microwave for 1-2 minutes or reheat on moderate heat in a skillet.

SPAGHETTI SQUASH WITH CHICKEN & TOMATO SAUCE

INGREDIENTS

- 200g skinless chicken breast, diced
- 1 small spaghetti squash
- ½ cup crushed tomatoes (no added sugar)
- ½ tsp garlic powder
- ¼ tsp black pepper
- ½ tsp dried basil
- 1 tbsp water

 PREP TIME: 15 MINS   **COOK TIME:** 25 MINS   **SERVING:** 2

INSTRUCTIONS

1. Cut the spaghetti squash in half, discard the seeds, and place cut-side down on a parchment-lined baking sheet. Bake for 20 minutes or until tender.
2. Heat a non-stick skillet on moderate heat. Add the diced chicken, garlic powder, black pepper, and dried basil. Cook for 6–7 minutes, stirring occasionally, until the chicken is fully cooked through.
3. Add crushed tomatoes to the skillet and let everything simmer for 3–4 minutes to combine flavors.
4. Scrape the baked spaghetti squash with a fork to create "noodles," and top with the chicken-tomato sauce before serving.

Nutrition

Calories: 190, **Fat:** 3g, **Cholesterol:** 45mg, **Carbohydrates:** 9g, **Sugar:** 3g, **Protein:** 30g, **Sodium:** 180mg, **Fiber:** 2g

Storage & Reheating:

Refrigeration: Store in an airtight container for up to 2 days.
Freezing: Not recommended.
Reheating: Microwave for 1-2 minutes.

BROCCOLI & TURKEY CASSEROLE

INGREDIENTS

- 150g lean ground turkey
- 1 cup broccoli florets, chopped
- ½ cup nonfat Greek yogurt (or unsweetened coconut yogurt for dairy-free)
- ½ tsp garlic powder
- ¼ tsp black pepper
- ½ tsp dried thyme

PREP TIME: 10 MINS   **COOK TIME:** 20 MINS   **SERVING:** 2

INSTRUCTIONS

1. Preheat oven to 375°F (190°C).
2. Heat a non-stick skillet on moderate heat and toss in the ground turkey. Cook for 5-6 minutes, breaking it apart as it browns.
3. Stir in the broccoli and cook for more 3 minutes until slightly tender.
4. Remove from the stove flame and mix in Greek yogurt, garlic powder, black pepper, and thyme.
5. Transfer the mixture to the paper-arranged baking dish and bake for 10 minutes until golden.
6. Serve warm and enjoy!

Nutrition
Calories: 190, **Fat:** 3g, **Cholesterol:** 50mg, **Carbohydrates:** 7g, **Sugar:** 2g, **Protein:** 32g, **Sodium:** 180mg, **Fiber:** 2g

Storage & Reheating:

Refrigeration: Store in an airtight container for up to 3 days.
Freezing: Freeze for up to 2 months.
Reheating: Microwave for 1-2 minutes or reheat on moderate heat in a skillet.

HERB-CRUSTED BAKED TILAPIA WITH CAULIFLOWER MASH

INGREDIENTS

- 200g tilapia fillet
- 1 cup cauliflower florets
- ½ tsp garlic powder
- ¼ tsp black pepper
- ½ tsp dried oregano
- 1 tbsp lemon juice
- 1 tbsp water

PREP TIME: 10 MINS	**COOK TIME:** 20 MINS	**SERVING:** 2

INSTRUCTIONS

1. Preheat oven to 375°F (190°C).
2. Massage the tilapia with garlic powder, black pepper, oregano, and lemon juice.
3. Place on the paper-arranged baking sheet and bake for 15 minutes until golden and flaky.
4. Meanwhile, steam cauliflower in a pot with 1 tbsp water for 5 minutes, until soft.
5. Mash cauliflower with a fork and season with black pepper before serving alongside the tilapia.

Nutrition
Calories: 180, **Fat:** 3g, **Cholesterol:** 50mg, **Carbohydrates:** 6g, **Sugar:** 2g, **Protein:** 32g, **Sodium:** 160mg, **Fiber:** 2g

Storage & Reheating:

Refrigeration: Store in an airtight container for up to 2 days.
Freezing: Not recommended.
Reheating: Microwave for 1-2 minutes.

LEMON PEPPER GRILLED CHICKEN WITH CABBAGE SLAW

INGREDIENTS

- 200g skinless chicken breast
- 1 cup cabbage, shredded
- ½ tsp garlic powder
- ¼ tsp black pepper
- ½ tsp dried dill
- 1 tbsp lemon juice
- 1 tbsp apple cider vinegar

PREP TIME: 10 MINS   **COOK TIME:** 12 MINS   **SERVING:** 2

INSTRUCTIONS

1. Massage the chicken breast with garlic powder, black pepper, and lemon juice. Let it sit for 5 minutes.
2. Heat a non-stick skillet on moderate heat. Grill the chicken for 6-7 minutes on one side until golden brown and fully cooked.
3. Grab the shallow bowl and toss in the shredded cabbage with apple cider vinegar and dill.
4. Slice the grilled meat and serve over the cabbage slaw.

Nutrition

Calories: 190, **Fat:** 2g, **Cholesterol:** 50mg, **Carbohydrates:** 6g, **Sugar:** 2g, **Protein:** 34g, **Sodium:** 170mg, **Fiber:** 2g

Storage & Reheating:

Refrigeration: Store in an airtight container for up to 2 days.
Freezing: Not recommended.
Reheating: Microwave for 1-2 minutes or reheat on moderate heat in a skillet.

ZUCCHINI NOODLES WITH LEAN GROUND TURKEY

INGREDIENTS

- 150g lean ground turkey
- 1 cup zucchini, spiralized
- ½ tsp garlic powder
- ¼ tsp black pepper
- ½ tsp dried basil
- 1 tbsp lemon juice
- 1 tbsp water

PREP TIME: 15 MINS **COOK TIME:** 12 MINS **SERVING:** 2

INSTRUCTIONS

1. Heat a non-stick skillet on moderate heat and toss in the ground turkey. Cook for 5-6 minutes, breaking it apart as it browns.
2. Sprinkle with garlic powder, black pepper, and basil, stirring well.
3. Add zucchini noodles and 1 tbsp water, then cook for more 3 minutes, stirring at intervals.
4. Drizzle with lemon juice and serve immediately.

Nutrition

Calories: 180, **Fat:** 2g, **Cholesterol:** 45mg, **Carbohydrates:** 6g, **Sugar:** 2g, **Protein:** 32g, **Sodium:** 160mg, **Fiber:** 2g

Storage & Reheating:

Refrigeration: Store in an airtight container for up to 2 days.
Freezing: Not recommended.
Reheating: Microwave for 1-2 minutes or reheat on moderate heat in a skillet.

BAKED TURKEY MEATBALLS WITH ROASTED ASPARAGUS

INGREDIENTS

- 150g lean ground turkey
- ½ cup cauliflower rice
- 1 cup asparagus, trimmed
- ½ tsp garlic powder
- ¼ tsp black pepper
- ½ tsp dried oregano
- 1 tbsp lemon juice

PREP TIME: 10 MINS
COOK TIME: 18 MINS
SERVING: 2

INSTRUCTIONS

1. Preheat oven to 375°F (190°C).
2. Grab the shallow bowl and mix ground turkey, cauliflower rice, garlic powder, black pepper, and oregano.
3. Form into small meatballs and place on an arranged baking sheet.
4. Arrange asparagus on the same sheet and drizzle with lemon juice.
5. Bake for 15-18 minutes, until meatballs are golden and cooked through.
6. Serve immediately with roasted asparagus.

Nutrition
Calories: 190, **Fat:** 3g, **Cholesterol:** 50mg, **Carbohydrates:** 7g, **Sugar:** 2g, **Protein:** 32g, **Sodium:** 180mg, **Fiber:** 2g

Storage & Reheating:

Refrigeration: Store in an airtight container for up to 3 days.
Freezing: Freeze meatballs for up to 2 months.
Reheating: Microwave for 1-2 minutes or reheat on moderate heat in a skillet.

ZESTY LEMON PEPPER FISH WITH ROASTED CAULIFLOWER

INGREDIENTS

- 200g white fish fillet (tilapia or cod)
- 1 cup cauliflower florets
- 1 tbsp lemon juice
- ½ tsp garlic powder
- ¼ tsp black pepper
- ½ tsp dried dill
- 1 tbsp water

PREP TIME: 10 MINS

COOK TIME: 15 MINS

SERVING: 2

INSTRUCTIONS

1. Preheat oven to 375°F (190°C).
2. Massage the fish fillet with lemon juice, garlic powder, black pepper, and dill.
3. Place fish and cauliflower florets on the paper-arranged baking sheet.
4. Roast for 12-15 minutes until the fish is flaky and cauliflower is tender.
5. Serve warm with roasted cauliflower.

Nutrition

Calories: 180, **Fat:** 3g, **Cholesterol:** 50mg, **Carbohydrates:** 6g, **Sugar:** 2g, **Protein:** 32g, **Sodium:** 160mg, **Fiber:** 2g

Storage & Reheating:

Refrigeration: Store in an airtight container for up to 2 days.
Freezing: Not recommended.
Reheating: Microwave for 1-2 minutes.

SAVORY CHICKEN & MUSHROOM SKILLET

INGREDIENTS

- 200g skinless chicken breast, diced
- 1 cup mushrooms, sliced
- ½ tsp garlic powder
- ¼ tsp black pepper
- ½ tsp dried thyme
- 1 tbsp water

 PREP TIME: 10 MINS   **COOK TIME:** 12 MINS   **SERVING:** 2

INSTRUCTIONS

1. Heat a non-stick skillet on moderate heat and toss in the diced chicken. Cook for 5-6 minutes, stirring at intervals, until lightly golden.
2. Add mushrooms and 1 tbsp water, then cook for more 5 minutes, stirring at intervals.
3. Sprinkle with garlic powder, black pepper, and thyme, stirring well.
4. Cook more for 2 minutes, allowing flavors to blend.
5. Serve immediately and enjoy!

Nutrition
Calories: 180, **Fat:** 2g, **Cholesterol:** 50mg, **Carbohydrates:** 5g, **Sugar:** 2g, **Protein:** 34g, **Sodium:** 160mg, **Fiber:** 1g

Storage & Reheating:

Refrigeration: Store in an airtight container for up to 3 days.
Freezing: Freeze for up to 2 months.
Reheating: Microwave for 1-2 minutes or reheat on moderate heat in a skillet.

MUSTARD GLAZED CHICKEN WITH ZUCCHINI MEDLEY

INGREDIENTS

- 200g skinless chicken breast
- 1 cup zucchini, diced
- 1 tbsp Dijon mustard (sugar-free)
- ½ tsp garlic powder
- ¼ tsp black pepper
- ½ tsp dried oregano
- 1 tbsp water

 PREP TIME: 10 MINS   **COOK TIME:** 15 MINS   **SERVING:** 2

INSTRUCTIONS

1. Massage the chicken breast with Dijon mustard, garlic powder, black pepper, and oregano. Let it sit for 5 minutes.
2. Heat a non-stick skillet on moderate heat and grill the chicken for 6-7 minutes on one side until golden brown and fully cooked.
3. In the same pan, toss in zucchini with 1 tbsp water and cook for 5 minutes, stirring at intervals.
4. Serve the chicken with the zucchini medley on the side.

Nutrition

Calories: 190, **Fat:** 3g, **Cholesterol:** 50mg, **Carbohydrates:** 6g, **Sugar:** 2g, **Protein:** 34g, **Sodium:** 170mg, **Fiber:** 2g

Storage & Reheating:

Refrigeration: Store in an airtight container for up to 2 days.
Freezing: Not recommended.
Reheating: Microwave for 1-2 minutes or reheat on moderate heat in a skillet.

DRINKS

CABBAGE & CUCUMBER DETOX JUICE

INGREDIENTS

- 1 cup green cabbage, chopped
- 1 medium cucumber, sliced
- ½ lemon, juiced
- 1 cup cold water
- ¼ tsp black pepper (optional)

PREP TIME: 5 MINS	**COOK TIME:** 00 MINS	**SERVING:** 2

INSTRUCTIONS

1. Blend the cabbage with cucumber, lemon juice, and water in a powerful food blender until smooth.
2. Strain the mixture (discard any pulp or solids) for a smoother texture.
3. Ladle into a glass, sprinkle with black pepper if desired, and serve fresh.

Nutrition
Calories: 25, **Fat:** 0g, **Cholesterol:** 0mg, **Carbohydrates:** 5g, **Sugar:** 2g, **Protein:** 1g, **Sodium:** 20mg, **Fiber:** 1g

Storage & Serving:

Refrigeration: Store in a sealed jar for up to 24 hours. Shake before drinking.

Freezing: Not recommended.

NONFAT YOGURT & STRAWBERRY PROTEIN SHAKE

INGREDIENTS

- 1 cup nonfat Greek yogurt (or unsweetened coconut yogurt for dairy-free)
- ½ cup strawberries, fresh or frozen
- 1 cup cold water
- ½ tsp vanilla extract (optional)

 PREP TIME: 5 MINS   **COOK TIME:** 00 MINS   **SERVING:** 2

INSTRUCTIONS

1. Grab the powerful food blender and throw in all the ingredients.
2. Blend them on full power until the mixture gets a smooth and creamy texture.
3. Ladle into a glass and serve immediately.

Nutrition
Calories: 100, **Fat:** 1g, **Cholesterol:** 5mg, **Carbohydrates:** 9g, **Sugar:** 5g, **Protein:** 14g, **Sodium:** 50mg, **Fiber:** 1g

Storage & Serving:

Refrigeration: Store in a sealed jar for up to 1 day. Shake before drinking.

Freezing: Not recommended.

UNSWEETENED HIBISCUS ICED TEA WITH LEMON

INGREDIENTS

- 2 tbsp dried hibiscus flowers
- 2 cups water
- ½ lemon, juiced
- Ice cubes (optional)

 PREP TIME: 5 MINS   **COOK TIME:** 10 MINS   **SERVING:** 2

INSTRUCTIONS

1. Boil 2 cups water in a shallow pot, then remove from the stove flame.
2. Add hibiscus flowers in hot water and leave them to steep for 10 minutes.
3. Strain the tea (to discard any solids) and let it cool to room temperature.
4. Add lemon juice and stir well, then serve over ice.

Storage & Serving:

Refrigeration: Store in an airtight container for up to 3 days.
Freezing: Not recommended.

Nutrition
Calories: 5, **Fat:** 0g, **Cholesterol:** 0mg, **Carbohydrates:** 1g, **Sugar:** 0g, **Protein:** 0g, **Sodium:** 5mg, **Fiber:** 0g

SPINACH & CUCUMBER GREEN JUICE

INGREDIENTS

- 1 cup fresh spinach
- 1 medium cucumber, sliced
- ½ lemon, juiced
- 1 cup cold water

PREP TIME: 5 MINS | **COOK TIME:** 00 MINS | **SERVING:** 2

INSTRUCTIONS

1. In a food blender, throw in all ingredients (spinach to cold water).
2. Blend on full power until the mixture gets a smooth texture.
3. Strain the mixture (to disard any solids or pulp) to get a smoother texture.
4. Ladle into a glass and serve immediately.

Nutrition
Calories: 20, **Fat:** 0g, **Cholesterol:** 0mg, **Carbohydrates:** 4g, **Sugar:** 1g, **Protein:** 1g, **Sodium:** 15mg, **Fiber:** 1g

Storage & Serving:

Refrigeration: Store in an airtight container for up to 24 hours.
Freezing: Not recommended.

HERBAL LEMON-GINGER DETOX TEA

INGREDIENTS

- 2 cups water
- 1 tsp grated fresh ginger
- ½ lemon, juiced
- ½ tsp dried chamomile (optional)

 PREP TIME: 5 MINS   **COOK TIME:** 10 MINS   **SERVING:** 2

INSTRUCTIONS

1. Boil 2 cups water in a shallow pot and add grated ginger.
2. Simmer for 5 minutes, then remove from the stove flame.
3. Stir in lemon juice and chamomile (if using).
4. Strain and serve warm.

Nutrition
Calories: 5, **Fat:** 0g, **Cholesterol:** 0mg, **Carbohydrates:** 1g, **Sugar:** 0g, **Protein:** 0g, **Sodium:** 5mg, **Fiber:** 0g

Storage & Serving:

Refrigeration: Store in an airtight container for up to 2 days.
Freezing: Not recommended.

60-DAY MEAL PLAN

WEEK 1

	BREAKFAST	LUNCH	DINNER	DRINK
DAY 1	Egg Whites with Spinach & Tomatoes (220 kcal, Page 11)	Grilled Chicken Salad with Lemon Vinaigrette (350 kcal, Page 32)	Baked Lemon Chicken with Cauliflower Rice (400 kcal, Page 58)	Cabbage & Cucumber Detox Juice (50 kcal, Page 79)
DAY 2	Zucchini & Egg White Frittata (240 kcal, Page 13)	Broccoli & Turkey Soup (340 kcal, Page 37)	Lemon Pepper Grilled Chicken with Cabbage Slaw (420 kcal, Page 72)	Spinach & Cucumber Green Juice (50 kcal, Page 82)
DAY 3	Low-Carb Cottage Cheese Pancakes (250 kcal, Page 18)	Grilled Tilapia with Spinach & Lemon Dressing (360 kcal, Page 50)	Herb-Crusted Baked Tilapia with Cauliflower Mash (400 kcal, Page 71)	Unsweetened Hibiscus Iced Tea with Lemon (10 kcal, Page 81)
DAY 4	Unsweetened Hibiscus Iced Tea with Lemon (10 kcal, Page 81)	Spicy Ground Turkey & Broccoli Bowl (350 kcal, Page 51)	Savory Chicken & Mushroom Skillet (400 kcal, Page 76)	Herbal Lemon-Ginger Detox Tea (5 kcal, Page 83)
DAY 5	Asparagus & Tomato Egg Muffins (250 kcal, Page 20)	Grilled Chicken & Cucumber Lettuce Wraps (340 kcal, Page 48)	Zesty Lemon Pepper Fish with Roasted Cauliflower (400 kcal, Page 75)	Cabbage & Cucumber Detox Juice (50 kcal, Page 79)
DAY 6	Nonfat Greek Yogurt with Cinnamon & Berries (260 kcal, Page 12)	Baked Turkey Meatballs with Roasted Asparagus (360 kcal, Page 74)	Roasted Salmon with Lemon & Zucchini (400 kcal, Page 65)	Nonfat Yogurt & Strawberry Protein Shake (100 kcal, Page 80)
DAY 7	Lean Turkey Breakfast Hash (210 kcal, Page 15)	Low-Carb Ground Turkey Lettuce Tacos (350 kcal, Page 67)	Mustard Glazed Chicken with Zucchini Medley (420 kcal, Page 77)	Spinach & Cucumber Green Juice (50 kcal, Page 82)

WEEK 1 SHOPPING LIST

PROTEINS & DAIRY
- [ ] Chicken breasts (4 boneless, skinless)
- [ ] Salmon fillets (2, 4 oz each)
- [ ] Lean beef (6 oz, sliced)
- [ ] Ground turkey (½ pound)
- [ ] Large shrimp (10, peeled & deveined)
- [ ] Eggs (4 large)
- [ ] Low-fat cottage cheese (1 cup)
- [ ] Greek yogurt (1 cup)
- [ ] Feta cheese (¼ cup)
- [ ] Plant-based protein powder (½ scoop)

Grains & Legumes
- [ ] Whole-wheat pasta (1 cup)
- [ ] Brown rice (½ cup dry)
- [ ] Quinoa (½ cup dry)
- [ ] Lentils (½ cup dry)
- [ ] Chickpeas (½ cup dry, soaked overnight)
- [ ] Whole-wheat couscous (½ cup dry)
- [ ] Kidney beans (½ cup dry, soaked overnight)
- [ ] Whole-wheat crackers (8)
- [ ] Whole-wheat tortillas (2)
- [ ] Rolled oats (½ cup)

Vegetables & Fruits
- [ ] Cucumber (1 small)
- [ ] Fresh spinach (1 cup)
- [ ] Mixed greens (2 cups)
- [ ] Cherry tomatoes (1 cup)
- [ ] Carrots (1 cup, diced)
- [ ] Celery (½ cup, diced)
- [ ] Zucchini (½ cup, diced)
- [ ] Bell peppers (½ cup, diced)
- [ ] Broccoli florets (1 cup)
- [ ] Red onion (½ cup, finely chopped)
- [ ] Blueberries (½ cup)
- [ ] Apple (1 medium)
- [ ] Banana (1 medium)
- [ ] Avocado (½)
- [ ] Strawberries (½ cup)

Pantry & Condiments
- [ ] Olive oil
- [ ] Balsamic vinegar
- [ ] Lemon juice
- [ ] Oregano
- [ ] Cumin
- [ ] Minced garlic
- [ ] Honey
- [ ] Vanilla extract

WEEK 2

	BREAKFAST	LUNCH	DINNER	DRINK
DAY 1	Zucchini & Egg White Breakfast Muffins (240 kcal, Page 28)	Steamed Fish with Asparagus & Vinegar Dressing (340 kcal, Page 44)	Spaghetti Squash with Chicken & Tomato Sauce (400 kcal, Page 69)	Unsweetened Hibiscus Iced Tea with Lemon (10 kcal, Page 81)
DAY 2	Lean Turkey & Cauliflower Hash (250 kcal, Page 17)	Nonfat Cottage Cheese & Cucumber Protein Plate (350 kcal, Page 63)	Baked Turkey & Zucchini Meatloaf (400 kcal, Page 62)	Herbal Lemon-Ginger Detox Tea (5 kcal, Page 83)
DAY 3	Low-Carb Greek Chicken Salad (260 kcal, Page 47)	Cabbage Stir-Fry with Garlic Shrimp (360 kcal, Page 66)	Oven-Baked Fish with Garlic & Herbs (400 kcal, Page 68)	Cabbage & Cucumber Detox Juice (50 kcal, Page 79)
DAY 4	High-Protein Scrambled Tofu Bowl (230 kcal, Page 21)	Grilled Turkey & Mushroom Skewers (350 kcal, Page 57)	Roasted Tilapia with Cabbage & Herb Dressing (400 kcal, Page 54)	Spinach & Cucumber Green Juice (50 kcal, Page 82)
DAY 5	Spaghetti Squash & Lean Chicken Hash (260 kcal, Page 22)	Broccoli & Turkey Casserole (360 kcal, Page 70)	Baked Turkey Meatballs with Roasted Asparagus (400 kcal, Page 74)	Nonfat Yogurt & Strawberry Protein Shake (100 kcal, Page 80)
DAY 6	Garlic Mushroom & Egg White Stir-Fry (240 kcal, Page 23)	Zucchini Noodles with Lean Ground Turkey (350 kcal, Page 73)	Lemon Garlic Baked Cod with Broccoli (400 kcal, Page 53)	Unsweetened Hibiscus Iced Tea with Lemon (10 kcal, Page 81)
DAY 7	Steamed Broccoli & Scrambled Tofu Plate (230 kcal, Page 29)	Baked Turkey & Zucchini Meatloaf (350 kcal, Page 62)	Mustard Glazed Chicken with Zucchini Medley (420 kcal, Page 77)	Herbal Lemon-Ginger Detox Tea (5 kcal, Page 83)

WEEK 2 SHOPPING LIST

Proteins
- [ ] 5 skinless chicken breasts
- [ ] 500g lean ground turkey
- [ ] 3 tilapia or cod fillets
- [ ] 2 salmon fillets
- [ ] 6 egg whites
- [ ] 1 pack smoked salmon
- [ ] 2 cups nonfat cottage cheese
- [ ] 1 cup nonfat Greek yogurt

Vegetables
- [ ] 5 cups spinach
- [ ] 3 medium zucchinis
- [ ] 2 large cucumbers
- [ ] 1 head cabbage
- [ ] 3 cups cherry tomatoes
- [ ] 2 bell peppers
- [ ] 3 cups broccoli florets
- [ ] 1 small spaghetti squash
- [ ] 1 head cauliflower
- [ ] 1 bunch asparagus
- [ ] 2 cups mushrooms

Pantry & Spices
- [ ] 1 tbsp Dijon mustard (sugar-free)
- [ ] 1 tbsp apple cider vinegar
- [ ] 2 tbsp dried oregano
- [ ] 1 tbsp dried basil
- [ ] 1 tsp black pepper
- [ ] 1 tsp garlic powder

Drinks & Miscellaneous
- [ ] 1 cup hibiscus flowers (for tea)
- [ ] 1 ginger root
- [ ] 2 lemons
- [ ] 1 cup strawberries

WEEK 3

	BREAKFAST	LUNCH	DINNER	DRINK
DAY 1	Cottage Cheese & Cucumber Protein Bowl (240 kcal, Page 25)	Grilled Fish with Lemon & Steamed Veggies (350 kcal, Page 40)	Garlic & Herb Turkey Meatballs (400 kcal, Page 61)	Unsweetened Hibiscus Iced Tea with Lemon (10 kcal, Page 81)
DAY 2	Low-Carb Cottage Cheese Pancakes (250 kcal, Page 18)	Broccoli & Turkey Soup (340 kcal, Page 37)	Baked Lemon Chicken with Cauliflower Rice (400 kcal, Page 58)	Herbal Lemon-Ginger Detox Tea (5 kcal, Page 83)
DAY 3	Smoked Salmon & Egg White Scramble (230 kcal, Page 19)	Turkey & Spinach Stuffed Bell Peppers (350 kcal, Page 39)	Roasted Salmon with Lemon & Zucchini (400 kcal, Page 65)	Cabbage & Cucumber Detox Juice (50 kcal, Page 79)
DAY 4	Zucchini & Egg White Breakfast Muffins (240 kcal)	Lemon Herb Turkey Skewers with Zucchini (360 kcal)	Herb-Crusted Baked Tilapia with Cauliflower Mash (400 kcal)	Spinach & Cucumber Green Juice (50 kcal
DAY 5	Baked Egg Whites with Herbs & Veggies (240 kcal, Page 24)	Lemon Herb Turkey Skewers with Zucchini (360 kcal, Page 43)	Herb-Crusted Baked Tilapia with Cauliflower Mash (400 kcal, Page 71)	Spinach & Cucumber Green Juice (50 kcal, Page 82)
DAY 6	Spaghetti Squash & Lean Chicken Hash (260 kcal, Page 22)	Low-Carb Ground Turkey Lettuce Tacos (350 kcal, Page 67)	Baked Turkey Meatballs with Roasted Asparagus (400 kcal, Page 74)	Unsweetened Hibiscus Iced Tea with Lemon (10 kcal, Page 81)
DAY 7	Spaghetti Squash & Lean Chicken Hash (260 kcal, Page 22)	Low-Carb Ground Turkey Lettuce Tacos (350 kcal, Page 67)	Baked Turkey Meatballs with Roasted Asparagus (400 kcal, Page 74)	Herbal Lemon-Ginger Detox Tea (5 kcal)

WEEK 3 SHOPPING LIST

Proteins
- [ ] 6 skinless chicken breasts
- [ ] 500g lean ground turkey
- [ ] 3 tilapia or cod fillets
- [ ] 3 salmon fillets
- [ ] 6 egg whites
- [ ] 2 cups nonfat cottage cheese
- [ ] 2 cups nonfat Greek yogurt

Vegetables
- [ ] 5 cups spinach
- [ ] 3 zucchinis
- [ ] 2 large cucumbers
- [ ] 1 head cabbage
- [ ] 3 cups cherry tomatoes
- [ ] 2 bell peppers
- [ ] 3 cups broccoli florets
- [ ] 1 small spaghetti squash
- [ ] 1 head cauliflower
- [ ] 1 bunch asparagus
- [ ] 2 cups mushrooms

Pantry & Spices
- [ ] 1 tbsp Dijon mustard (sugar-free)
- [ ] 1 tbsp apple cider vinegar
- [ ] 2 tbsp dried oregano
- [ ] 1 tbsp dried basil
- [ ] 1 tsp black pepper
- [ ] 1 tsp garlic powder

Drinks & Miscellaneous
- [ ] 1 cup hibiscus flowers (for tea)
- [ ] 1 ginger root
- [ ] 2 lemons
- [ ] 1 cup strawberries

WEEK 4

	BREAKFAST	LUNCH	DINNER	DRINK
DAY 1	Garlic Mushroom & Egg White Stir-Fry (240 kcal, Page 23)	Spicy Ground Turkey & Broccoli Bowl (350 kcal, Page 51)	Oven-Baked Fish with Garlic & Herbs (400 kcal, Page 68)	Cabbage & Cucumber Detox Juice (50 kcal, Page 79)
DAY 2	Lean Turkey Breakfast Hash (210 kcal, Page 15)	Steamed Fish with Asparagus & Vinegar Dressing (340 kcal, Page 44)	oasted Tilapia with Cabbage & Herb Dressing (400 kcal, Page 54)	Spinach & Cucumber Green Juice (50 kcal, Page 82)
DAY 3	Nonfat Greek Yogurt with Cinnamon & Berries (260 kcal, Page 12)	Broccoli & Turkey Casserole (360 kcal, Page 70)	Garlic & Herb Turkey Meatballs (400 kcal, Page 61)	Unsweetened Hibiscus Iced Tea with Lemon (10 kcal, Page 81)
DAY 4	Cottage Cheese & Cucumber Protein Bowl (240 kcal, Page 25)	Turkey & Spinach Stuffed Bell Peppers (350 kcal, Page 39)	Zesty Lemon Pepper Fish with Roasted Cauliflower (400 kcal, Page 75)	Herbal Lemon-Ginger Detox Tea (5 kcal, Page 83)
DAY 5	Steamed Broccoli & Scrambled Tofu Plate (230 kcal, Page 29)	Grilled Chicken & Cucumber Lettuce Wraps (340 kcal, Page 48)	Mustard Glazed Chicken with Zucchini Medley (420 kcal, Page 77)	Nonfat Yogurt & Strawberry Protein Shake (100 kcal, Page 80)
DAY 6	Low-Carb Cottage Cheese Pancakes (250 kcal, Page 18)	Baked Turkey & Zucchini Meatloaf (350 kcal, Page 62)	Herb-Crusted Baked Tilapia with Cauliflower Mash (400 kcal, Page 71)	Unsweetened Hibiscus Iced Tea with Lemon (10 kcal, Page 81)
DAY 7	Egg Whites with Spinach & Tomatoes (220 kcal, Page 11)	Cabbage Stir-Fry with Garlic Shrimp (360 kcal, Page 66)	Roasted Salmon with Lemon & Zucchini (400 kcal, Page 65)	Cabbage & Cucumber Detox Juice (50 kcal, Page 79)
BONUS DAY	Egg Whites with Spinach & Tomatoes (220 kcal, Page 11)	Cabbage Stir-Fry with Garlic Shrimp (360 kcal, Page 66)	Roasted Salmon with Lemon & Zucchini (400 kcal, Page 65)	Cabbage & Cucumber Detox Juice (50 kcal, Page 79)
BONUS DAY	Egg Whites with Spinach & Tomatoes (220 kcal, Page 11)	Cabbage Stir-Fry with Garlic Shrimp (360 kcal, Page 66)	Roasted Salmon with Lemon & Zucchini (400 kcal, Page 65)	Cabbage & Cucumber Detox Juice (50 kcal, Page 79)

WEEK 4 SHOPPING LIST

Proteins
- [ ] 5 skinless chicken breasts
- [ ] 500g lean ground turkey
- [ ] 3 tilapia or cod fillets
- [ ] 2 salmon fillets
- [ ] 6 egg whites
- [ ] 2 cups nonfat cottage cheese
- [ ] 2 cups nonfat Greek yogurt

Vegetables
- [ ] 5 cups spinach
- [ ] 3 zucchinis
- [ ] 2 large cucumbers
- [ ] 1 head cabbage
- [ ] 3 cups cherry tomatoes
- [ ] 2 bell peppers
- [ ] 3 cups broccoli florets
- [ ] 1 small spaghetti squash
- [ ] 1 head cauliflower
- [ ] 1 bunch asparagus
- [ ] 2 cups mushrooms

Pantry & Spices
- [ ] 1 tbsp Dijon mustard (sugar-free)
- [ ] 1 tbsp apple cider vinegar
- [ ] 2 tbsp dried oregano
- [ ] 1 tbsp dried basil
- [ ] 1 tsp black pepper
- [ ] 1 tsp garlic powder

Drinks & Miscellaneous
- [ ] 1 cup hibiscus flowers (for tea)
- [ ] 1 ginger root
- [ ] 2 lemons
- [ ] 1 cup strawberries

WEEK 5

	BREAKFAST	LUNCH	DINNER	DRINK
DAY 1	Cottage Cheese & Cucumber Protein Bowl (240 kcal, Page 25)	Tuna & Cucumber Salad with Mustard Dressing (350 kcal, Page 38)	Lean Chicken Stir-Fry with Bok Choy (400 kcal, Page 56)	Cabbage & Cucumber Detox Juice (50 kcal, Page 79)
DAY 2	Zucchini & Egg White Breakfast Muffins (240 kcal, Page 28)	Turkey Lettuce Wraps with Mustard (340 kcal, Page 33)	Low-Carb Turkey & Cabbage Slaw Stir-Fry (400 kcal, Page 55)	Spinach & Cucumber Green Juice (50 kcal, Page 82)
DAY 3	Lean Turkey Breakfast Hash (210kcal, Page 15)	Cauliflower & Lean Chicken Stir-Fry (350 kcal, Page 34)	Roasted Tilapia with Cabbage & Herb Dressing (400 kcal, Page 54)	Unsweetened Hibiscus Iced Tea with Lemon (10 kcal, Page 81)
DAY 4	Baked Egg Whites with Herbs & Veggies (240 kcal, Page 24)	Lemon Herb Turkey Skewers with Zucchini (360 kcal)	Herb-Crusted Baked Tilapia with Cauliflower Mash (400 kcal)	Spinach & Cucumber Green Juice (50 kcal
DAY 5	Lean Turkey & Cauliflower Hash (250 kcal, Page 17)	Cauliflower Rice Sushi with Lean Tuna (350 kcal, Page 45)	Spaghetti Squash & Shrimp Bowl (400 kcal, Page 59)	Cabbage & Cucumber Detox Juice (50 kcal, Page 79)
DAY 6	Garlic Mushroom & Egg White Stir-Fry (240 kcal, Page 23)	Turkey & Spinach Stuffed Bell Peppers (350 kcal, Page 39)	Grilled Turkey & Mushroom Skewers (400 kcal, Page 57)	Spinach & Cucumber Green Juice (50 kcal, Page 82)
DAY 7	High-Protein Scrambled Tofu Bowl (230 kcal, Page 21)	Low-Carb Greek Chicken Salad (360 kcal, Page 47)	Roasted Salmon with Lemon & Zucchini (400 kcal, Page 65)	Nonfat Yogurt & Strawberry Protein Shake (100 kcal, Page 80)

WEEK 5 SHOPPING LIST

Proteins
- [ ] Skinless chicken breasts (5 pieces)
- [ ] Lean ground turkey (400g)
- [ ] Tuna (canned in water) (2 cans)
- [ ] Tilapia fillets (2 fillets)
- [ ] Salmon fillets (2 fillets)
- [ ] Shrimp (peeled and deveined) (300g)
- [ ] Egg whites (carton or 14 eggs)
- [ ] Nonfat Greek yogurt (2 cups)
- [ ] Nonfat cottage cheese (2 cups)

Vegetables
- [ ] Broccoli (3 heads)
- [ ] Zucchini (5 medium)
- [ ] Bok choy (2 heads)
- [ ] Cauliflower (1 large)
- [ ] Cherry tomatoes (2 cups)
- [ ] Cucumbers (4 large)
- [ ] Mushrooms (2 cups sliced)
- [ ] Cabbage (2 heads)
- [ ] Spinach (5 cups)
- [ ] Asparagus (1 bunch)

Pantry & Spices
- [ ] Dijon mustard (sugar-free)
- [ ] Apple cider vinegar
- [ ] Olive oil spray
- [ ] Garlic powder
- [ ] Onion powder
- [ ] Black pepper
- [ ] Dried oregano
- [ ] Dried basil
- [ ] Drinks & Miscellaneous
- [ ] Hibiscus flowers (for tea)
- [ ] Fresh ginger
- [ ] Lemons (6)
- [ ] Strawberries (1 cup)

WEEK 6

	BREAKFAST	LUNCH	DINNER	DRINK
DAY 1	Asparagus & Tomato Egg Muffins (250 kcal, Page 20)	Tuna & Cucumber Salad with Mustard Dressing (350 kcal, Page 38)	Baked Turkey Meatballs with Roasted Asparagus (400 kcal, Page 74)	Herbal Lemon-Ginger Detox Tea (5 kcal, Page 83)
DAY 2	Cottage Cheese & Cucumber Protein Bowl (240 kcal, Page 25)	Steamed Shrimp with Zucchini & Garlic Sauce (340 kcal, Page 49)	Oven-Baked Fish with Garlic & Herbs (400 kcal, Page 68)	Spinach & Cucumber Green Juice (50 kcal, Page 82)
DAY 3	Zucchini & Egg White Frittata (240 kcal, Page 13)	Grilled Tilapia with Spinach & Lemon Dressing (350 kcal, Page 50)	Lemon Garlic Baked Cod with Broccoli (400 kcal, Page 53)	Unsweetened Hibiscus Iced Tea with Lemon (10 kcal, Page 81)
DAY 4	Nonfat Greek Yogurt with Cinnamon & Berries (260 kcal, Page 12)	Broccoli & Turkey Soup (340 kcal, Page 37)	Baked Turkey & Zucchini Meatloaf (400 kcal, Page 62)	Cabbage & Cucumber Detox Juice (50 kcal, Page 79)
DAY 5	Steamed Broccoli & Scrambled Tofu Plate (230 kcal, Page 29)	Zucchini Noodles with Garlic & Shrimp (350 kcal, Page 36)	Mustard Glazed Chicken with Zucchini Medley (420 kcal, Page 77)	Spinach & Cucumber Green Juice (50 kcal, Page 82)
DAY 6	Garlic Mushroom & Egg White Stir-Fry (240 kcal, Page 23)	Turkey Lettuce Wraps with Mustard (340 kcal, Page 33)	Herb-Crusted Baked Tilapia with Cauliflower Mash (400 kcal, Page 71)	Herbal Lemon-Ginger Detox Tea (5 kcal, Page 83)
DAY 7	Cottage Cheese & Cucumber Protein Bowl (240 kcal, Page 25)	Cabbage Slaw with Grilled Chicken Strips (350 kcal, Page 41)	Baked Lemon Chicken with Cauliflower Rice (400 kcal, Page 58)	Nonfat Yogurt & Strawberry Protein Shake (100 kcal, Page 80)

WEEK 6 SHOPPING LIST

Proteins
- [ ] Skinless chicken breasts (5 pieces)
- [ ] Lean ground turkey (400g)
- [ ] Tilapia fillets (3 fillets)
- [ ] Cod fillets (2 fillets)
- [ ] Shrimp (300g)
- [ ] Egg whites (carton or 14 eggs)
- [ ] Nonfat Greek yogurt (2 cups)
- [ ] Nonfat cottage cheese (2 cups)

Vegetables
- [ ] Broccoli (3 heads)
- [ ] Zucchini (5 medium)
- [ ] Cauliflower (1 large)
- [ ] Cherry tomatoes (2 cups)
- [ ] Cabbage (2 heads)
- [ ] Spinach (4 cups)
- [ ] Mushrooms (2 cups sliced)
- [ ] Asparagus (1 bunch)
- [ ] Cucumbers (3 large)

Pantry & Spices
- [ ] Dijon mustard (sugar-free)
- [ ] Apple cider vinegar
- [ ] Olive oil spray
- [ ] Garlic powder
- [ ] Onion powder
- [ ] Black pepper
- [ ] Dried oregano
- [ ] Dried basil
- [ ] Drinks & Miscellaneous
- [ ] Hibiscus flowers (for tea)
- [ ] Fresh ginger
- [ ] Lemons (6)
- [ ] Strawberries (1 cup)

WEEK 7

	BREAKFAST	LUNCH	DINNER	DRINK
DAY 1	Low-Carb Cottage Cheese Pancakes (250 kcal, Page 18)	Lemon Herb Turkey Skewers with Zucchini (360 kcal, Page 43)	Garlic & Herb Turkey Meatballs (400 kcal, Page 61)	Cabbage & Cucumber Detox Juice (50 kcal, Page 79)
DAY 2	Lean Turkey Breakfast Hash (210 kcal, Page 15)	Grilled Chicken & Cucumber Lettuce Wraps (340 kcal, Page 48)	Low-Carb Turkey & Cabbage Slaw Stir-Fry (400 kcal, Page 55)	Spinach & Cucumber Green Juice (50 kcal, Page 82)
DAY 3	Zucchini & Egg White Breakfast Muffins (240 kcal, Page 28)	Cauliflower & Lean Chicken Stir-Fry (350 kcal, Page 34)	Spaghetti Squash with Chicken & Tomato Sauce (400 kcal, Page 69)	Unsweetened Hibiscus Iced Tea with Lemon (10 kcal, Page 81)
DAY 4	High-Protein Scrambled Tofu Bowl (230 kcal, Page 21)	Broccoli & Turkey Casserole (360 kcal, Page 70)	Mustard Glazed Chicken with Zucchini Medley (420 kcal, Page 77)	Herbal Lemon-Ginger Detox Tea (5 kcal, Page 83)
DAY 5	Cottage Cheese & Cucumber Protein Bowl (240 kcal, Page 25)	Steamed Shrimp with Zucchini & Garlic Sauce (340 kcal, Page 49)	Roasted Salmon with Lemon & Zucchini (400 kcal, Page 65)	Nonfat Yogurt & Strawberry Protein Shake (100 kcal, Page 80)
DAY 6	Garlic Mushroom & Egg White Stir-Fry (240 kcal, Page 23)	Tuna & Cucumber Salad with Mustard Dressing (350 kcal, Page 38)	Baked Turkey Meatballs with Roasted Asparagus (400 kcal, Page 74)	Cabbage & Cucumber Detox Juice (50 kcal, Page 79)
DAY 7	Zucchini & Egg White Frittata (240 kcal, Page 13)	Lemon Herb Turkey Skewers with Zucchini (360 kcal, Page 43)	Lemon Pepper Grilled Chicken with Cabbage Slaw (420 kcal, Page 72)	Spinach & Cucumber Green Juice (50 kcal, Page 82)

WEEK 7 SHOPPING LIST

Proteins
- [ ] Skinless chicken breasts (6 pieces)
- [ ] Lean ground turkey (400g)
- [ ] Tilapia fillets (2 fillets)
- [ ] Salmon fillets (2 fillets)
- [ ] Shrimp (300g)
- [ ] Egg whites (carton or 14 eggs)
- [ ] Nonfat Greek yogurt (2 cups)
- [ ] Nonfat cottage cheese (2 cups)

Vegetables
- [ ] Broccoli (3 heads)
- [ ] Zucchini (5 medium)
- [ ] Cauliflower (1 large)
- [ ] Cabbage (2 heads)
- [ ] Mushrooms (2 cups sliced)
- [ ] Asparagus (1 bunch)
- [ ] Cherry tomatoes (2 cups)
- [ ] Spinach (5 cups)
- [ ] Cucumbers (3 large)

Pantry & Spices
- [ ] Dijon mustard (sugar-free)
- [ ] Apple cider vinegar
- [ ] Olive oil spray
- [ ] Garlic powder
- [ ] Onion powder
- [ ] Black pepper
- [ ] Dried oregano
- [ ] Dried basil
- [ ] Drinks & Miscellaneous
- [ ] Hibiscus flowers (for tea)
- [ ] Fresh ginger
- [ ] Lemons (6)
- [ ] Strawberries (1 cup)

WEEK 8

	BREAKFAST	LUNCH	DINNER	DRINK
DAY 1	Low-Carb Cottage Cheese Pancakes (250 kcal, Page 18)	Cabbage Slaw with Grilled Chicken Strips (350 kcal, Page 41)	Herb-Crusted Baked Tilapia with Cauliflower Mash (400 kcal, Page 71)	Unsweetened Hibiscus Iced Tea with Lemon (10 kcal, Page 81)
DAY 2	Nonfat Greek Yogurt with Cinnamon & Berries (260 kcal, Page 12)	Grilled Fish with Lemon & Steamed Veggies (350 kcal, Page 40)	Garlic & Herb Turkey Meatballs (400 kcal, Page 61)	Herbal Lemon-Ginger Detox Tea (5 kcal, Page 83)
DAY 3	Steamed Broccoli & Scrambled Tofu Plate (230 kcal, Page 29)	Broccoli & Turkey Soup (340 kcal, Page 37)	Baked Lemon Chicken with Cauliflower Rice (400 kcal, Page 58)	Cabbage & Cucumber Detox Juice (50 kcal, Page 79)
DAY 4	Cottage Cheese & Cucumber Protein Bowl (240 kcal, Page 25)	Grilled Tilapia with Spinach & Lemon Dressing (350 kcal, Page 50)	Mustard Glazed Chicken with Zucchini Medley (420 kcal, Page 77)	Spinach & Cucumber Green Juice (50 kcal, Page 82)
DAY 5	Garlic Mushroom & Egg White Stir-Fry (240 kcal, Page 23)	Tuna & Cucumber Salad with Mustard Dressing (350 kcal, Page 38)	Roasted Tilapia with Cabbage & Herb Dressing (400 kcal, Page 54)	Nonfat Yogurt & Strawberry Protein Shake (100 kcal, Page 80)
DAY 6	Lean Turkey Breakfast Hash (210 kcal, Page 15)	Turkey Lettuce Wraps with Mustard (340 kcal, Page 33)	Garlic & Herb Turkey Meatballs (400 kcal, Page 61)	Herbal Lemon-Ginger Detox Tea (5 kcal, Page 83)
DAY 7	Low-Carb Cottage Cheese Pancakes (250 kcal, Page 18)	Cabbage Stir-Fry with Garlic Shrimp (360 kcal, Page 66)	Oven-Baked Fish with Garlic & Herbs (400 kcal, Page 68)	Cabbage & Cucumber Detox Juice (50 kcal, Page 79)
BONUS DAY	Zucchini & Egg White Breakfast Muffins (240 kcal, Page 28)	Turkey & Spinach Stuffed Bell Peppers (350 kcal, Page 39)	Roasted Salmon with Lemon & Zucchini (400 kcal, Page 65)	Spinach & Cucumber Green Juice (50 kcal, Page 82)
BONUS DAY	Cottage Cheese & Cucumber Protein Bowl (240 kcal, Page 25)	Lemon Herb Turkey Skewers with Zucchini (360 kcal, Page 43)	Lemon Pepper Grilled Chicken with Cabbage Slaw (420 kcal, Page 72)	Herbal Lemon-Ginger Detox Tea (5 kcal, Page 83)

WEEK 8 SHOPPING LIST

Proteins
- [ ] Skinless chicken breasts (5 pieces)
- [ ] Lean ground turkey (400g)
- [ ] Tilapia fillets (3 fillets)
- [ ] Cod fillets (2 fillets)
- [ ] Shrimp (300g)
- [ ] Salmon fillets (2 fillets)
- [ ] Egg whites (carton or 14 eggs)
- [ ] Nonfat Greek yogurt (2 cups)
- [ ] Nonfat cottage cheese (2 cups)

Vegetables
- [ ] Broccoli (3 heads)
- [ ] Zucchini (5 medium)
- [ ] Cabbage (2 heads)
- [ ] Cauliflower (1 large)
- [ ] Spinach (5 cups)
- [ ] Mushrooms (2 cups sliced)
- [ ] Cucumbers (4 large)
- [ ] Cherry tomatoes (2 cups)
- [ ] Asparagus (1 bunch)

Pantry & Spices
- [ ] Dijon mustard (sugar-free)
- [ ] Apple cider vinegar
- [ ] Olive oil spray
- [ ] Garlic powder
- [ ] Onion powder
- [ ] Black pepper
- [ ] Dried oregano
- [ ] Dried basil
- [ ] Drinks & Miscellaneous
- [ ] Hibiscus flowers (for tea)
- [ ] Fresh ginger
- [ ] Lemons (6)
- [ ] Strawberries (1 cup)

Recipes Index

A

Asparagus & Tomato Egg Muffins 20

B

Baked Egg Whites with Herbs & Veggies 24
Baked Lemon Chicken with Cauliflower Rice 58
Baked Turkey Meatballs with Roasted Asparagus 74
Baked Turkey & Zucchini Meatloaf 62
Broccoli & Egg White Bake 16
Broccoli & Turkey Casserole 70
Broccoli & Turkey Soup 37

C

Cabbage & Cucumber Detox Juice 79
Cabbage & Mushroom Omelet 14
Cabbage Slaw with Grilled Chicken Strips 41
Cabbage Stir-Fry with Garlic Shrimp 66
Cauliflower & Lean Chicken Stir-Fry 34
Cauliflower Rice Porridge with Nonfat Yogurt 30
Cauliflower Rice Sushi with Lean Tuna 45
Cottage Cheese & Cucumber Protein Bowl 25

E

Egg Whites with Spinach & Tomatoes 11

G

Garlic & Herb Turkey Meatballs 61
Garlic Mushroom & Egg White Stir-Fry 23
Grilled Chicken & Cucumber Lettuce Wraps 48
Grilled Chicken Salad with Lemon Vinaigrette 32
Grilled Fish with Lemon & Steamed Veggies 40
Grilled Tilapia with Spinach & Lemon Dressing 50
Grilled Tomato & Nonfat Cottage Cheese Bowl 27
Grilled Turkey & Mushroom Skewers 57

H

Herbal Lemon-Ginger Detox Tea 83
Herb-Crusted Baked Tilapia with Cauliflower Mash 71
High-Protein Scrambled Tofu Bowl 21

L

Lean Chicken & Cabbage Spring Rolls 64
Lean Chicken Stir-Fry with Bok Choy 56
Lean Turkey & Bell Pepper Breakfast Wrap 26
Lean Turkey & Cauliflower Hash 17
Lemon Garlic Baked Cod with Broccoli 53
Lemon Herb Turkey Skewers with Zucchini 43
Lemon Pepper Grilled Chicken with Cabbage Slaw 72
Low-Carb Cottage Cheese Pancakes 18
Low-Carb Greek Chicken Salad 47
Low-Carb Ground Turkey Lettuce Tacos 67
Low-Carb Turkey & Cabbage Slaw Stir-Fry 55

M

Mushroom & Tofu Stir-Fry with Garlic 42
Mustard Glazed Chicken with Zucchini Medley 77

N

Nonfat Cottage Cheese & Cucumber Protein Plate 63
Nonfat Greek Yogurt with Cinnamon & Berries 12
Nonfat Yogurt & Strawberry Protein Shake 80

O

Oven-Baked Fish with Garlic & Herbs 68

R

Roasted Salmon with Lemon & Zucchini 65
Roasted Tilapia with Cabbage & Herb Dressing 54

S

Savory Chicken & Mushroom Skillet 76
Smoked Salmon & Egg White Scramble 19
Spaghetti Squash & Lean Chicken Hash 22
Spaghetti Squash & Shrimp Bowl 59
Spaghetti Squash with Chicken & Tomato Sauce 69
Spicy Egg White & Mushroom Scramble Bowl 35
Spicy Ground Turkey & Broccoli Bowl 51
Spinach & Cucumber Green Juice 82
Steamed Broccoli & Scrambled Tofu Plate 29
Steamed Fish with Asparagus & Vinegar Dressing 60
Steamed Shrimp with Zucchini & Garlic Sauce 49
Steamed Tilapia with Spinach & Vinegar Dressing 44

T

Lean Turkey Breakfast Hash 15
Tuna & Cucumber Salad with Mustard Dressing 38
Turkey Lettuce Wraps with Mustard 33
Turkey & Spinach Stuffed Bell Peppers 39

U

Unsweetened Hibiscus Iced Tea with Lemon 81

Z

Zesty Grilled Shrimp with Cabbage Slaw 46
Zesty Lemon Pepper Fish with Roasted Cauliflower 75
Zucchini & Egg White Breakfast Muffins 28
Zucchini & Egg White Frittata 13
Zucchini Noodles with Garlic & Shrimp 36
Zucchini Noodles with Lean Ground Turkey 73

Made in United States
Cleveland, OH
02 August 2025